P9-CDN-285

PARIS

MACMILLAN AND CO., Limited
LONDON · BOMBAY · CALCUTTA · MADRAS
MELBOURNE

THE MACMILLAN COMPANY
NEW YORK · BOSTON CHICAGO
DALLAS · SAN FRANCISCO

THE MACMILLAN CO. OF CANADA, Ltd.
TORONTO

THE PALAIS DU SENAT

PARIS

BY

SIDNEY DARK

AUTHOR OF "LONDON"

WITH DRAWINGS

BY

HENRY RUSHBURY

A.R.W.S.

MACMILLAN AND CO., LIMITED

ST. MARTIN'S STREET, LONDON

1926

PRINTED IN GREAT BRITAIN
BY R. & R. CLARK, LIMITED, EDINBURGH

CONTENTS

ILLUSTRATIONS

FOREWORD

When I wrote my *London* I felt it necessary to apologise for the addition of another volume to a well-stocked library, and if explanation was demanded for the appearance of that book, it may be not unreasonably suggested that it is even more obviously required for the publication of this companion volume on Paris. There is already a very wilderness of books in English concerned with the French capital from one point of view or another.

Paris is a city so crammed with interest, so varied and exciting in the impressions that it offers, that each explorer must of necessity make discoveries for himself. Every man's Paris is his own, with its own characteristics, and is in some respects at least unlike the Paris of any one else.

My book is nothing more than a series of personal impressions. I have made no sort of attempt to be comprehensive. As in *London* I have met the ghosts who attract me, and, following my habit in the material world, I have avoided the ghosts who bore me. As with my *London*, I have been fortunate enough to count as a collaborator an artist of original and outstanding talent, and his pictures may be regarded by the critics as some compensation for the text.

Every great city has its characteristic note. London is good-humoured. Before the War, Berlin was certainly bumptious. Rome always seems to me a city of tremendous dignity. And Paris is a city of experience, and of the disillusionment that is generally the result of experience. The Parisian is of all men the most sophisticated. Paris is a city of realists, unaffected by sentimentality ; a city of industry and thrift ; a city of irony, but rarely of laughter, of wit but never of humour, of superficial tolerance and yet of a people who regard the rest of the world with more or less amiable contempt.

Paris is the city of good food, drink that really cheers, men that intrigue and women that fascinate. It is because I have earned my living in Paris that I have come to know it, but none the less all cities have a certain fascination that is lost with too intimate a knowledge. Of all the women in the world the Parisian woman is the best to look at. When one knows her one discovers that she is not quite so different from other women as one would have supposed from the way that she does her hair. The discovery is something of a shock, but with it all, woman is the chief ornament of Paris as she is the chief industrial asset of France. I recall Swinburne's translation of Villon's ballad :

> Prince, give praise to our French ladies
>   For the sweet sound of their speaking carries ;
> 'Twixt Rome and Cadiz many a maid is
>   But no good girl's lip out of Paris.

Incidentally, and the fact, unimportant though it is, explains why this book has been written, Paris is the city that I love. I do not think it is properly called *la ville lumière*, indeed I should call it *la ville triste*. I do not think that its people are notable for their courtesy, for I have many times watched elderly gentlemen boarding crowded trains on the *Métro* with the aid of the points of their umbrellas.

I know little of that peculiar life of Paris which attracts the tourist and which the Parisian, being a realist and fond of money, provides in the night restaurants of Montmartre. On the other hand, it has been my fortune, and it is an experience that falls to comparatively few foreigners, to be on terms of friendship and some intimacy, not only with

French men, but also with French families. I think I know the French for what they are and not for what admiring ignorance or racial prejudice believes that they are, and on the whole I find them very good.

I am immensely indebted to my friends, Mr. and Mrs. George Adam, for their kindness in reading my proofs.

SIDNEY DARK.

July 1926.

I

SOUTHWARD FROM THE MADELEINE

Standing on the steps of the Madeleine one looks downhill along the Rue Royale across the Place de la Concorde and the Pont de la Concorde to the Chambre des Députés. A church is at the top of the hill and a parliament at the bottom. But lest too much should be deduced from this fact, it should be added that the church itself was originally built by Napoleon as a temple of glory in which the memory of his victories might be kept alive. Its site was a graveyard, where the victims of the guillotine were hastily buried. Here were brought, among others, the bodies of Charlotte Corday and Marie Antoinette, and it is said that among the records in the Madeleine is an entry by the sexton: "Paid seven francs for a coffin for the widow Capet." After the fall of Napoleon, and before the building was finished, it became a church. Marie Antoinette was reinterred at St. Denis. To me the Madeleine is unimpressive and dull, betraying its pagan origin. But it is pleasant to stand on its steps in the summer, with the flower markets on either hand, and to look towards the famous Place, and the river beyond.

I have one vivid personal memory of the Madeleine. I arrived in Paris late one evening in January 1915, when the horror of the war had not been lessened by familiarity. Paris was a dark city. Hardly a street lamp was alight. And, as I passed the Madeleine, scores of sombrely clothed men and women, who had been praying for the repose of the souls of their dead, came down the long flight of stone steps, almost like spectres, to be lost in the darkness of the surrounding streets. It was my first realisation of the tragedy of war. England's losses at that time had been comparatively slight, and though it was not my last or worst close experience of war sorrow, the picture will always remain with me.

Opposite the Madeleine, at the corner of the Rue Royale and the Grands Boulevards, was the famous Restaurant Durand. It was at Durand's that General Boulanger, a pinchbeck militarist adventurer, met with his friends to decide whether or no to attempt a *coup d'État*. If it had been attempted it would probably have been a success, and Boulanger, whose black horse and threats to Germany and attacks on the parliamentary system which the French people have never loved, had made him a popular hero, would have been a dictator. But Boulanger was a coward. The moment passed, and he went into exile to commit suicide two years afterwards in Brussels. Boulanger was the hero of the music-halls, and the great Paulus, the most famous of French café chantant singers, made his own reputation and the adventurer's with the now forgotten "En revenant de la Revue."

There is little history in the Rue Royale though (and this is, may be, to be preferred) there are many excellent restaurants. Among them I count most highly the Restaurant Weber where, for a moderate figure, the wise can dine well, and indeed far better than at the more fashionable eating-places, that cater for the tourists with over-filled purses. At Weber the discerning always drink Vouvray, that delightful *vin de Touraine* which, as a punishment for the sins of the English, high Heaven will not permit to travel without deterioration.

It was at number eight Rue Royale that Madame de Staël lived at the end of her life, being moved from there in the summer of 1817 to die in the Rue Neuve des Mathurins. The indomitable woman, whom Napoleon feared more than any of his enemies, fought death with splendid courage. She was threatened with paralysis, but she declined to change her mode of life. "She resisted the attack with heroic imperturbability: invited everywhere, going everywhere, keeping open house, receiving in the morning, at dinner and in the evening, all the distinguished men of all parties, ranks and stations, taking the same interest in politics, literature, philosophy and society whether serious or frivolous, intimate or noisy, of the Government or of the Opposition, as in the brightest days of her early youth."

Few men or women have crammed so much experience into fifty-one years as Madame de Staël, the daughter of Necker, the Swiss banker-minister of Louis XVI. She had sat as a small girl, upright on a high chair, listening to the wisdom that fell from the lips of the encyclopædists. Diderot, d'Alembert, Grimm, Gibbon and Hume were among the celebrities with whom she was familiar, and Grimm copied out her childish essays and circulated them among his friends. She was the greatest figure of the period of sensibility. It is jolly to remember that she journeyed all the way to London to weep on the tomb of Richardson, whose *Clarissa* had touched her heart. Her novels were vastly applauded in her own time though they are now forgotten. Mme. de Staël was a great woman—a *grande amoureuse*, a tremendous traveller, an enthusiastic hater. Byron, whom she met in Italy, asserted that she talked too much, while she said of the English poet that he had "just enough sensibility to ruin a woman's happiness." Of all the stories of Mme. de Staël I like best the incident of her calling on Barras in the days of the Directoire to demand that Talleyrand, who was credited with being one of her many lovers, should be made Minister of Foreign Affairs, weepingly protesting that if Barras refused, the ex-bishop of Autun would throw himself into the Seine !

The Place de la Concorde at the bottom of the Rue Royale has been the scene of many of the most thrilling events in the history of France. At the left-hand corner is the Ministère de la Marine, from the balcony of which, with a group of Senators and Deputies, I watched President Wilson make his triumphal entry into Paris in December 1918, the legislators ironically shouting, *Vivent les quatorze points*, as the American President bowed right and left with uncomfortable wooden dignity. On the right-hand corner is the Hotel Crillon where the Americans had their headquarters during the Peace Congress. On the left the Tuileries gardens, on the right the Champs-Élysées, and in front the river and the Chambre des Députés.

The Place de la Concorde was first laid out as a square in the middle of the eighteenth century. Louis XV., popular as all young kings are when they succeed the aged and decrepit, was taken dangerously ill at Metz. To his people he was then the Well-Beloved, and the whole nation prayed for his recovery. "The prayers of priests and people," wrote a contemporary quoted by Carlyle, "were every moment interrupted by their sobs." The Well-Beloved recovered, and, as a thank-offering, the people of Paris determined to erect a statue to their King. The site selected was then a stretch of market gardens between the Tuileries and the river, and the Place was created very much as it is now. The statue of the King showed him crowned with laurels and riding a charger, surrounded by four figures of the Virtues. It was twenty-one years before the whole design was completed and by that time the Well-Beloved had become the Generally Hated. As Carlyle says: "With Pompadourism and Du Barryism, his *fleur de lis* has been shamefully struck down in all lands and on all seas." And Paris laughed when it saw the king on his charger with the Virtues at his feet:

> Ah la belle statue, oh le beau piédestal,
> Les Vertus sont à pied et les Vices à cheval!

In 1770 Paris was *en fête* on the occasion of the marriage of the Dauphin to Marie Antoinette. A display of fireworks was given on the Place Louis Quinze, as it was then called, and one of the rockets was discharged directly into the crowd, causing a wild panic. Many of the sightseers were pushed into the river and were drowned. Others attempted to escape by the Rue Royale, which was obstructed by new building operations, and were crushed underfoot, and more than a hundred were killed there—an omen of the hapless lot of the royal pair.

At the Revolution the Place Louis Quinze became the Place de la Révolution. The statue of the King who "opened his mouth, said nothing and thought not at all," gave place to a statue of Liberty, and on the east side, almost in front of the gates that nowadays admit to the Tuileries gardens, the guillotine was set up in 1793. Guillotin, who has given his name to the instrument of death, demanded at the Constitutional Assembly that, as a democratic right "in all cases of capital punishment it shall be of the same kind—that is decapitation—and that it shall be executed by means of a machine." Under the old

PLACE DE LA CONCORDE

régime only men of noble birth had the right to have their heads cut off. For lowlier persons there was the gibbet and the rope. But all men were to be equal in the Republic, both in life and in death. The first guillotine was constructed under the direction of the Secretary of the Academy of Surgeons, and before it was used for the hated aristocrats, experiment was made on a highwayman in the Place de Grève.

The guillotine was erected on the Place de la Révolution, particularly for the execution of Louis XVI. History has no more pathetic figure. He is more pathetic than Mary Queen of Scots or Charles I., or any other of the kings and queens whose life has ended with a violent death, because he was so harmless and so extraordinarily futile. Mary and Charles, and even Marie Antoinette in her way, had played their parts, but Louis was nothing but the victim of his times. Carlyle has told the story of his execution in some of the most masterly passages in a peerless book. It was a great scene, lacking nothing in intensity and dignity, and culminating with the Abbé Edgeworth's splendid command : " *Fils de St. Louis, montez au Ciel!* "

For a year the guillotine was taken to the Place du Carrousel, but it was back again in the Place de la Révolution for the killing of Charlotte Corday, that appealing revolutionary figure who appears on the stage only to disappear ; of Madame Roland, a type of the sententious doctrinaire who contrives revolutions, always to be destroyed by them ; and of Queen Marie Antoinette, guilty of nothing but of being beautiful and frivolous and a queen—offences grave enough, be it added, at a time of a nation's rebirth. She was a good mother and, so far as was possible with dull Louis, a good wife, but Anatole France has some justification when he says that she was " frivolous, ignorant, imprudent, light-headed and extravagant, and that, as Queen of France, she had an anti-French policy." To the French people she was always the Austrian, and the pro-Austrian policy that she compelled her husband's Government to adopt was one of the causes of her undoing.

These were the three most notable of the twelve hundred and thirty-five victims of Sanson, the headsman, a sufficiently large number, but a small exploit in massacre compared to the achievements of the Russian Bolshevists. If the world has seen progress nowhere else, it has certainly seen progress in revolutionary zeal. The Revolution took over many of the officials of the Bourbon Government, among them the headsman. The notorious Sanson belonged to a family of executioners, and when he retired after the Terror he was succeeded by his son, who retained his office under the Directoire, the Consulate and the Empire, and during the reigns of Louis XVIII., Charles X. and Louis Philippe. Sanson was a serious, conscientious tradesman as may be gathered from the following curious letter that he wrote to Fouquier-Tinville :

Au citoyen Fouquier, accusateur public du tribunal révolutionnaire, Paris.

CITOYEN—Suivant les ordres que j'ai reçus du département de faire construire des panières, etc., se trouvant sur le point d'estre faits, et ses sortes de marchandises, ne pouvant se trouver confondues avec les charpentes sans courir le risque d'estre à chaque instant écrasés, il reste à côté du angard que vous avez fait donner au charpentier un autre petit angard propre à mettre deux voitures. Il sera sufisant mais nécessaire pour le service des exécutions attandu que ces paniers seront montés sur des roues. L'exécuteur vous prie, citoyen, de vouloir bien lui faire donner ce local pour les objets détaillés cy-dessus, d'ailleurs il n'y aura pas de dépense à faire cy ce n'est l'élargissement de la porte qui consistera à lever deux planches.

Le citoyen républicain
SANSON.
exécuteur des jugements criminels à Paris.

Paris, ce 25 floréal l'an 2 de la République une et indivisible.

It is hard to understand the enjoyment that the guillotine gave to revolutionary Paris. It is hard to comprehend the mentality of Madame Defarge and her friends, who sat in the front seats, knitting and counting the heads as they fell into the basket. But it is well to remember that executions outside Newgate Gaol remained a popular amusement long after the revolutionary Terror had run its course in Paris.

It was in the evening of April 5, 1794, while the setting sun burnished the statue of Liberty in the centre of the square, that the Republic destroyed the greatest of its sons. Danton is the outstanding, splendid, masculine figure of the French Revolution. Heroic times do not necessarily call forth an army of heroic figures. It is indeed the irony of life that little men are constantly bungling great opportunities. But the French Revolution was, at its best, the work of two great men—Mirabeau and Danton. It was destroyed by a miserable little man—Robespierre. By the beginning of 1794 it was clear that Robespierre and Danton could not exist together, and it was the mean, acid plotter, aided by the fanatical eloquence of Saint-Just, " a youth of slight stature with mild mellow voice, enthusiast olive complexion and long black hair," who swayed the Convention and decreed a mock trial for Danton and the guillotine on the Place de la Révolution. The tumbrils came, from the prison of the Conciergerie, along the Rue St. Honoré, and as Danton and his friends passed the house of Duplay, where he lodged, they knew that Robespierre (Mr. Belloc has called him " the mad narrow enemy of mercy and of all good things ") was hidden behind the shutters.

So they arrived at the square, Danton massive, unafraid, buoying up the courage of his friends, taunting his enemy in satiric song, and at the end, the last to die, thinking of his wife and muttering to himself, " I shall never see her again. No weakness ! " Rarely in the whole history of the world have men witnessed so magnificent a passing into the unseen—a great figure, certain of himself, arrogant with justification. " I am Danton not unknown among the revolutionaries, I shall be living nowhere soon, but you will find my name in Valhalla ! "

Swift Nemesis ! Less than four months later Robespierre, with his broken jaw-bone done up in dirty linen, is jostled along the Rue St. Honoré on the same journey as his great enemy.

It was to his house at what is now the Rue Royale end of this street that Duplay, who is generally described as a carpenter, but who was really a comparatively comfortable bourgeois, took Robespierre in 1791, after he had made a hectic speech at the Jacobin Club, and when his life was in danger, during what proved to be a temporary and unimportant reaction. Robespierre lived with Duplay until his course was run, content in an atmosphere of unqualified adulation. It was a simple, sober household, and Robespierre was a simple, sober man, and yet as even a simple, sober man well may be, a creature of most excessive vanity, delighted always to see the full-length portrait of himself on the wall and his metal bust on the writing-table. It was from this house that he went out to fight for his life, neatly attired, wearing his famous light blue coat. Duplay, who was an intelligent politician, was fearful for the safety of his friend, but Robespierre had no foreboding. But again to quote Mr. Belloc, " he never came home and he never slept again." He died well hated. A woman in the crowd sprang up to the side of the cart and struck him in the face, and, always the victim of phrases, he muttered : " *De mourir pour le peuple et d'en être abhorré !* "

Robespierre is an enigma. To Carlyle he is the sea-green incorruptible, an honest dyspeptic, a narrow-souled doctrinaire. Mr. Belloc says that he could neither laugh nor hate. He was the high priest of the gospel of Rousseau, but he never understood that gospel. He was tireless, persistent, a peerless schemer. The death of Danton was in a sense the supreme achievement of his career, and its undoing. When Danton died no man was safe. It was in very truth the blood of Danton that choked Robespierre when he attempted to defend himself before his accusers.

The great crowd in the Place de la Révolution was awed and silent when Danton died. The scene was that of an epic tragedy. But when Robespierre died it was a tawdry melodrama, the crowd shouting execrations, the executioner brutally tearing off the bandage from his victim's broken jaw, the man howling in agony as he died.

Napoleon gave its present name to the square in 1799, using it for military displays, the demonstration to the Parisians of his victories and his glory. In 1815, after the surrender and exile of the Emperor, British troops bivouacked on the Place, the Duke of Wellington doubtless rejoicing that his long march with the insufferable Blücher had come to an end. The statue of Liberty was pulled down and carted away. The Bourbons were back in their ancient capital, but not for long. After the Revolution of 1830 the Citizen King erected in the centre of the Place the famous Luxor column given to him by the Sultan of Turkey, and it is there to this day.

1848, and another revolution ! The Citizen King, stealing out of the Tuileries, hired a cab on the Place de la

THE CHAMBRE DES DEPUTES

Concorde to take him on the first part of his journey to the exile that was the usual lot of France's nineteenth-century rulers.

It was in the Chambre des Députés, most uncomfortable of parliament houses, that the beginning of the Second Republic was decreed, a great cheering crowd swarming over the quays and bridge into the Place de la Concorde behind, with Alexandre Dumas among the Deputies who decided that France should have no more kings.

Twenty-two years pass, and on the 4th September 1870, there was again a great crowd on the Place, surging towards the Chamber. The news of the defeat at Sedan had reached the capital, the Second Empire had been found out, and Paris was demanding another change of ruler. Standing on a chair behind the railings Gambetta, the tribune of the people, black-bearded, olive-skinned, fiercely eloquent, urged them to patience and restraint. The always malicious Edmond de Goncourt says of Gambetta: "He has the fat and oily face of a money-changer on whom the gas of the Boulevard de l'Opéra shines by night." But he admitted that "this man who appears so child-like and sleepy has an attention always on the alert." The foreigner has played a large part in the history of France. Napoleon I. was an Italian in mind and by descent. Napoleon III. was more than half German, at least in culture. Gambetta was the son of a Genoese grocer, and it was he who inspired France with the courage to accept misfortune with dignity and to preserve her soul after her defeat by Germany. De Goncourt has left us an account of the proclamation of the Third Republic:

"Towards four o'clock the outside of the *Chambre* looked thus: Separating itself from the greyness of the façade, above and around the pillars, on the steps of the grand staircase, a multitude has accumulated, a world of men whose blouses make blue and white spots against the black-clothes men, the majority of whom have boughs in their hands or bouquets of green leaves fastened to their hats. Suddenly a hand raises itself above all the heads and writes on a pillar, in great red letters, the list of members of the Provisional Government, while, at the same time appears in black on another pillar, 'The Republic is Proclaimed.' Then shouts of applause, hats in the air, people climbing up the pedestals of the statues, a man in a blouse who calmly begins to smoke his pipe on the stone knees of the Chancellor L'Hôpital, and clusters of women who hang on to the railings immediately opposite the Pont de la Concorde."

The Parisians were so delighted at having got rid of Napoleon III. that "strangers met on the Place de la Concorde, shook hands warmly with each other and were happy enough to forget all about the war and the Germans."

Paris during the siege of 1870 was a city of fantasy, of courage and odd incidents, of despair clutching at every straw of hope. A great crowd of children was seen one morning, for example, singing and dancing on the Place de la Concorde around two sandy-haired Bavarian prisoners, guarded by a detachment of Gardes Mobiles. Two prisoners were taken! Paris might yet be saved!

Has any square in Europe such a treasure-house of thrilling memories? Here died Louis XVI. and Marie Antoinette; Charlotte Corday and Madame Roland; Danton and Robespierre. Here a king furtively hid himself in a four-wheeled cab. Here crowds have acclaimed the beginnings of two republics. Across the square has ridden a pinchbeck general on a black charger, for the moment a popular hero and almost made a dictator against his will, and in 1918 across the square there passed an austere professor from America intent on making the world safe for democracy.

II

WESTWARD FROM THE PLACE DE LA CONCORDE

THE view looking westward on a sunny morning from the Place du Carrousel, near the Louvre, is the best that Paris can offer and one that few other cities can rival. In a long unbroken line you see the Tuileries gardens, the Place de la Concorde and the Champs-Élysées, crowned with the Arc de Triomphe. Beyond, but out of sight, the line continues along the Avenue de la Grande Armée, the Porte Maillot and Neuilly. I know no more delightful adventure on such a sunny morning than to walk leisurely along the Champs-Élysées in the shade of the trees, and to conjure up the memories enshrined in this most wonderful avenue. It is a walk not without adventure, for the Paris taxi-driver takes the right-hand turn from the Place de la Concorde always at top speed, and in a manner that demonstrates his indifference to death—either his own or his passenger's or the wayfarer's.

Each man to his own taste, and I always linger longest at the Petit Guignol, the famous Punch and Judy shows on the right-hand side of the Avenue, which are the delight of the true Parisian from early youth to hoary age. Near the Petit Guignol there is on certain days of the week an open-air stamp market, and it is good to stop for a while watching the bargainings and exchanges. I have none of the zest of the collector. Spending money on used stamps seems to me sheer insanity, and it tickles my pride to see other people in deadly earnest over something that to me does not matter in the least.

The Champs-Élysées were first planned by Marie de Médicis in 1616, and her Cours la Reine still exists on the south side of the Avenue. Marie de Médicis was an unattractive, unpleasant and unhappy lady. Henri IV. owed money to the great family of Florentine bankers and married Marie to prevent them being too insistent in their demand for repayment. Marie was a bad bargain. "Imperious, jealous, stupid to a degree, ruled at all times by the dregs of the Court and by the people she had brought with her from Italy, she was the cause of wretchedness to Henri IV., to her son and to herself as well, though she might have been the happiest woman in Europe merely at the cost of abstaining from giving way to her temper and her servants." She was immensely fat, immensely stupid, and immensely lazy, and she pitted herself against Richelieu with the result that she spent the later part of her life in lonely exile. But during the years of her power, after the murder of Henri IV. in 1610, Marie, "the fat she-banker," as the Parisians called her, set her mark on Paris. She planned the Champs-Élysées, she built the Palais du Luxembourg and added to the Louvre. Incidentally she was the mother of Louis XIII. and of Henrietta Maria, the unfortunate wife of Charles I.

The tree-planted Avenue, as we know it now, dates from 1670, when Colbert, the dour minister of Louis XIV. found the money, while doubtless begrudging it. Colbert was a statesman born out of due season. He believed in the power of money. Had he been permitted, he would have made seventeenth-century France rich, and probably the Revolution would not have taken place—an unpleasant, hard, ill-mannered man this Colbert, the son of a small tradesman, and at the beginning of his life steward to Mazarin. Madame de Sévigné called him "the north," and his sour face and hollow eyes must have well suited the gloomy atmosphere of the Court of the Grand Monarque when he had repented of his sins and was tended by de Maintenon, even though it was said of Colbert that he "thought only of his finances and hardly ever of religion." In less austere days Colbert had gained favour by permitting his wife to bring up the children of La Vallière. Colbert created the French navy and developed French overseas trade. He carried on the great traditions of Richelieu by founding the Institut de France, the Observatoire and various academies. And in the manner of the

THE ARC DE TRIOMPHE

age, he enriched himself and his family. Be it added that he gave pensions to Molière, Corneille and Racine. This hard man—so odd is human nature—had one strange weakness. He took immense pains to prove a fictitious descent from the kings of Scotland. And I have often wondered, and never discovered, why *sole Colbert* is named after him. But perhaps it is not.

Marie de Médicis, fat and silly, Colbert, thin and clever, and Napoleon were the creators of the Champs-Élysées. It was Napoleon who crowned the Avenue with the Arc de Triomphe, erected as a monument to his glory. The Arc de Triomphe has on two sad occasions been an Arc d'Humilité. Through it there marched in 1815 the allied armies after Waterloo to bivouac on the Place de la Concorde. Through it in 1871 marched the conquering Germans, Paris being at last starved into submission, tramping along the Avenue watched by silent, half-fed men and women, already dreaming of *la revanche*. Their dreams came true. In the early autumn of 1919 I watched from the roof of the Hôtel Astoria the Victory March of the Allies through Napoleon's arch, justified at last, and along the tree-lined Avenue of a city that never lost its dignity during those years of trial, and now was elate with joy.

Under the Arc de Triomphe lies the body of the Unknown Soldier of France. The French borrowed the idea of immortalising a nameless hero-patriot from England, and who in England knows that the suggestion first came from an almost unknown army chaplain, the Rev. David Railton ?

Of all the processions that have passed up the Champs-Élysées, I like best to recall the progress of Queen Victoria and the Prince Consort in 1855. It was a return visit, Napoleon III. and Eugénie having stayed at Windsor some months before. The conquest of Victoria by Louis Napoleon was the great achievement of his career. He had to counter the prejudice of the proud heir of a long line of monarchs, who at first regarded him as an unscrupulous adventurer. But Napoleon knew how to manage women, even when they were swathed in English respectability. He talked to the Queen in his low, insinuating voice, and what was far more effective, he modestly and with respectful attention listened to Albert's ceaseless monologues. Only once did he show the slightest boredom, and that, as the Prince recorded, was "when I expatiated a little on the Holstein question." The Queen, in odd contrast to Eugénie's elegance, was dowdily dressed, but she won the hearts of bourgeois France by her bourgeois virtues. And not only bourgeois France. "*S'il y avait beaucoup de femmes comme elle*," said Béranger, "*je leur pardonnerais d'être reine*." And the elder Dumas regretted that he had not been given an audience. "*Une femme aussi remarquable et qui deviendra probablement la plus grande femme du siècle aurait dû se rencontrer avec le plus grand homme en France*." In a sense the *entente* may be said to have begun in these summer days in 1855 when Queen Victoria with husband and children stayed at St. Cloud and drove about the city. Waterloo was at last forgotten, even though elderly lookers-on might suggest that Napoleon I. would not have approved of the diplomatic triumph of Napoleon III. "*Si le vieux revenait, il serait rudement colère*."

Open-air restaurants and open-air music-halls with strident jazz tunes and energetic English dancers are to the right and left of the Avenue until one arrives at the Rond-Point near which, at number nine Avenue d'Antin, now Avenue Victor Emmanuel, lived Marguerite Gauthier, "La Dame aux Camélias." I have little sympathy with the sentimentalising of the courtesan, for which Alexandre Dumas *fils* was responsible, but none the less what memories he and Marguerite have contrived between them! I remember Coquelin and Sarah Bernhardt playing together in the Dumas play, Sarah of the wondrous voice, of whom even the disgruntled Edmond de Goncourt said: "This woman has undoubtedly an innate amiability, a desire to please which is not put on, but natural." And I recall a greater than Sarah—Eleonora Duse—as Marguerite, acting with a haughty austerity that made Dumas entirely ridiculous. Alphonsine Plessis was the real name of the woman whom Dumas made the heroine of his play. She was a beautiful Norman, always notably well dressed, as modest as it was possible for a woman in her position to be, and with her success she had the constant conviction that she was destined to die very young.

Close to the Rond-Point too, lived Madame Tallien, in a thatched cottage, and there, poverty-stricken, half blind and ill, her divorced husband, the redoubtable Thermidorist, died in 1820. The men of the Revolution nearly all died young. Tallien—" Clerk Tallien " as Carlyle calls him—outlived most of them, and he died when he was fifty-three, his active life having ceased twenty years before. Two events from his few years of power must have lived most vividly with him. It was in November 1793 that he was sent to Bordeaux to set up the guillotine and extirpate Girondism. It was there that he met the beautiful Thérèse, " a brown beautiful woman," the daughter of a Spanish merchant, who pleaded for her friends and contrived to soften the heart of the bristly fox-haired terrorist. It was she, " Our Lady of Thermidor," who urged him to plan the overthrow of Robespierre and the end of the Terror. Under the thatched roof of his wife's cottage—the brown Thérèse had become the Princesse de Chimay—he must often have repeated to himself with a little consoling pride his famous speech of July 1794 when, interrupting Saint-Just, he brandished a dagger and exclaimed, " If the Convention dare not strike the tyrant, then I myself dare."

After Thermidor, Tallien practically disappeared from the political stage, but Thérèse was the great lady of the Directoire. " Behold her," says Carlyle, " that beautiful adventurous *citoyenne* in costume of the ancient Greeks, such Greek as painter David could teach ; her sweeping tresses snooded by glittering antique fillet ; bright-dyed tunic of Greek women ; her little feet naked, as in antique statues with mere sandals and winding strips of ribbon defying the frost." It was she who introduced Josephine Beauharnais to Barras. She was present when Napoleon, unaccustomed to luxury, clumsy in manner and appearance, first met Josephine at Barras's house, and she urged Josephine to marry, when Barras, " tired and bored, was eager to find her a husband." Not a lady over whom moralists can wax enthusiastic, but " Our Lady of Thermidor," none the less, a woman who turned the heart of a revolutionist and hindered the activities of the guillotine.

Near by at number three Avenue Matignon, Heine died in 1856. The great German poet, the patriotic Jew who worshipped Napoleon because he had freed the Jews from their political disabilities, had been condemned for eight years to a mattress grave with a disease of the spine, tended faithfully by the uneducated, vain French shop-girl whom he had married, and writing wonderful poems inspired by his mystic passion for *Die Mouche*.

By far the most interesting house in the Champs-Élysées district is the Palais de l'Élysée in the Faubourg St. Honoré, the street of the British Embassy and curiosity shops, the prices of which are not for the slender purse. The Palais de l'Élysée, now the home of the Presidents of the Third Republic, where Félix Faure died and where Poincaré, the Lorrainer with the shrill high voice, lived during the war, was built in 1718, and in 1753, a year before her death, it passed into the possession of La Pompadour, the passionless courtesan whose domination over Louis XV. lasted long after his passion for her had ceased. La Pompadour was a woman of greed and brains, sufficiently a child of the eighteenth century to favour the philosophers, generally only to be snubbed by them. Voltaire called her "la Pompadounette," Rousseau wrote to her that "a charcoal-burner's wife was more to be respected than a king's mistress." La Pompadour died at Versailles, but her body was brought to the Palais de l'Élysée before it was interred in the vault of the Church of the Capucines on the site of the Place Vendôme. She was forty-three when she died. At the beginning of her reign, twenty years before, she was the subject of the famous scabrous Parisian jokes, the "Poissonnades," in which her lowly origin was ridiculed. One verse ran :

> Une petite bourgeoise,
> Élevée à la grivoise,
> Mesurant tout à sa toise,
> Fait de la cour un taudis—dis—dis,
> Louis, malgré son scrupule,
> Froidement pour elle brûle,
> Et son amour ridicule
> A fait rire tout Paris—ris—ris.

Later in the eighteenth century the Palais de l'Élysée was inhabited by the Duchesse de Bourbon, mother of the Duc d'Enghien, who was done to death by Napoleon. From 1803 to 1808 it was the home of Murat and Caroline Bonaparte. Murat, the son of an innkeeper, was the typical Napoleonic swashbuckler, the greatest of those first-class fighting men whom Arthur Conan Doyle has used with

BRITISH EMBASSY

such ingenuity in his *Brigadier Gerard.* He was with Napoleon in 1795 when they were both penniless soldiers in Paris. He was with him when the " whiff of grape shot " brought the Revolution to an end. He was with him in his first campaign in Italy, and he was with him in Egypt, leading the cavalry charge at the battle of the Pyramids. He was with him in Paris at the *coup d'État* of the 18th Brumaire. He commanded the cavalry at Marengo, at Austerlitz and at Jena, and in 1806 the innkeeper's son was made King of Naples. Napoleon's sisters were not lovable young women, and Caroline must have been the most difficult of them all. From the beginning they demanded their full share of their brother's loot, and Caroline was quite prepared to intrigue against him whenever she thought that she was not receiving hers. Made by the conqueror sovereigns of Naples, she and her husband assumed the arrogance of genuine royalty, and this brought down on them Napoleon's furious admonitions and denunciations of what he called their " monkey tricks." King Murat had ideas. He dreamed, as so many other men had dreamed since Cesare Borgia, of a united Italy, of course with himself as king. Somewhat against his will he joined Napoleon in the unfortunate Russian campaign, hastening home when disaster occurred, haply to save his throne. Subsequently he intrigued with Austria and England, and was used by them as a cat's-paw to be thrown over when the Bonaparte adventure had collapsed. During the Hundred Days he again offered his sword to Napoleon, but it was contemptuously refused, and the refusal was afterwards bitterly regretted, for Napoleon was convinced that with Murat at Waterloo, he would have won the battle. Afterwards, in a last insane and romantic adventure, Murat landed on the shores of Calabria, imagining that " his people " would welcome him. He was mistaken—and was imprisoned and shot. Caroline died in Trieste in 1838. Napoleon was not lucky in his relations, but Murat was at least picturesque, which is more than can be said for the stingy Joseph or the ill-tempered Louis. It is easy to imagine the gorgeous state in which he and Caroline lived in the Élysée when he was Governor of Paris in the halcyon days of the Empire.

The Élysée Palace is associated with Napoleon himself

in tragic times of his career. After the return from Elba and the public entry into the Tuileries, he moved to the Élysée for greater quiet, and there in the evening before he left Paris he dined alone with Hortense Beauharnais, one of the few who were always faithful to him, discussing the campaign that ended in Waterloo. He went back to the Élysée after the battle, and there he signed the act of abdication that was the prelude to the exile in St. Helena. The Élysée was offered to Josephine after the divorce, but she preferred Malmaison.

Between the First and Second Empire the Palais de l'Élysée was for a time occupied by the Duc de Bordeaux, grandson of Charles X., who might have been King of France had he not possessed to the full the Bourbon quality of learning nothing and forgetting nothing. Two years after the Franco-Prussian war, when Marshal MacMahon was President of the Republic, France was ready for a Bourbon restoration. The Duc de Berri, better known under the title of the Comte de Chambord, was the legitimate king, and had he been willing to abandon the *fleur de lis* for the tricolour, he might have been crowned in Rheims Cathedral.

Louis Napoleon lived at the Élysée after his election as Prince President of the Second Republic in 1848, and there the *coup d'État* was planned. Napoleon's half-brother, de Morny, a cynic and something of a wit, talking to his brother shortly before midnight on December 1, 1851, concerning the events which they had prepared, said to him : " Whatever happens during the next few hours, you are sure to have a sentry at your door to-morrow morning." De Morny was an intimate friend of Sarah Bernhardt's aunt, and, as such, was invited to attend a *conseil de famille* called to decide that lady's destiny when she was a girl at a convent school and was eager to take the veil. The future actress wept and implored, and her relations' hearts were moved by her apparent sincerity. When de Morny was asked for his opinion he said : " I will arrange for the young lady to begin her studies at the Conservatoire next week."

Napoleon's cousin, the Princess Mathilde, has left through Edmond de Goncourt a striking pen-picture of the Emperor, the veritable *roi fainéant* : " He is neither alive nor impressionable. Nothing bothers him. The other day a servant emptied a syphon of seltzer water down his neck, and he was quite satisfied with passing his glass across to the other side of him without saying a word or giving a single sign of impatience. A man who never gets into a temper and whose most irate expression is 'It's absurd.' He never says more than that. If I had married him I think I should have broken his head just to see what was inside."

On December 2, 1851, Louis Napoleon journeyed from the Élysée to the Tuileries. Eleven months afterwards a plebiscite approved the revolution. *Le paysan voulut couronner sa légende.* If Louis Napoleon had remained President, to quote Mr. Guedalla, "Maximilian would never have gone to Mexico or Bazaine to Metz, and the world would have missed the gas-lit tragedy of the Second Empire."

The Princess Mathilde lived in the Rue de Berri, a street running off the Champs-Élysées, in a house built by Mme. de Genlis, the famous educationist, who in the eighteenth century anticipated many of the theories of the twentieth. The Princess was the friend of all the great French writers of her time. She was a daughter of Jérôme Bonaparte and was the cleverest and the best of her family, as her father was the most rascally. She was a corpulent, dignified and sharp-tongued lady, whose salon was the centre of culture during her cousin's reign. She was most unhappily married to an unpleasant Russian from whom she separated sixty years before her death in 1904, and who was forced by the Czar Nicholas, who hated him and had great affection for her, to pay her a handsome allowance. I quote once again from the de Goncourts :

"This evening we are almost alone at the Princess's. She looks a little tired and talks about her past. She speaks about her marriage, Russia and the Emperor Nicholas. 'I shall never forgive you,' is what the Tsar said to her when she came to him, married to Demidov. The dream of the Tsar had been to give his son the hand of a Napoleon. So that this woman who was talking to us has missed two imperial crowns. Is it not natural that in her loneliness the memory of the shadow of the crowns which have all but touched her brows should come back to her ? "

My stroll along the Champs-Élysées is never quite complete without turning towards the river-side to look at the remarkable statue of Alphonse Daudet, as he has been called "Alphonse of the tired eyes." Nearly all the statues in London are an affront to high Heaven. Most of the statues in Paris are suggestive works of art. Perhaps, but I am not quite sure that it would be fair, the spiritual character of the two cities could be summarised and contrasted by the statue of Sir Wilfrid Lawson by the side of the Thames, and the statue of Alphonse Daudet by the side of the Seine.

Daudet was Scott's rival in industry. He would write from four o'clock in the morning till eight, from nine till twelve, from two till six, and from eight till midnight—twenty hours' work out of the twenty-four. Daudet was a great creator of characters, and his Tartarin is as real to me and nearly as jolly as Sam Weller himself. Daudet was a queer creature. Mistral, the poet of Provence, once described him as "the man of disillusion and of illusion, of a senile scepticism and a juvenile curiosity." Like many another famous writer he had a long spell of poverty before he achieved success, and in the de Goncourt *Journal* there is a delightful story, told by himself, of those early days :

"It was when I first began to write for the *Figaro*, when I was about seventeen. I don't know what was the matter, but one day I went to find Père Félix and asked him to confess me and to grant me absolution. He refused to do it unless I first read four large volumes of his sermons. Well, they were very nicely bound, and a few days later, when my access of religion had gone off a little, and being hungry, I sold the four volumes of Père Félix, which kept me in food for two or three days."

THE TUILERIES

III

THE TUILERIES

THERE are ghosts and to spare in the beautiful Tuileries gardens, east of the Place de la Concorde, with their trees and their statues and their subtle suggestion of that Parisian life which is unlike the life of any other city. Here in the summers of 1790 and 1791 a flaxen-haired small boy might have been seen walking with his mother or playing with his father, the passers-by regarding them with respect and almost with affection. He was the little Dauphin. It was in October 1789 that Louis XVI. came, against his will, from Versailles to the Tuileries Palace, which had for years been uninhabited and neglected. It was a tragic and menacing change. " Everything is dirty here, Mama," said the boy, and the King replied bitterly to the obsequious decorators and councillors who asked what alterations he suggested, " Each may lodge as he can. I am well enough." The royal family stayed for forty-one months at the Tuileries, guarded by Lafayette. They were months of illusion, when men still thought that revolutions could be peaceful and constitutional.

Disillusionment had come by the summer of 1792 when a tricolour ribbon was stretched across the gardens, marking the boundary between what was royal and what was national. The royal part, satirically called Coblentz, was generally empty and silent. Admission was only obtainable with a ticket of entry, and the ticket-holders were vastly suspected by patriotic Republicans. Inside the palace there were constant plottings for the escape of the King; Louis always hesitating when the time for action approached. He had made one attempt in the summer before, the famous flight to Varennes, only to be brought back to Paris, passing through silent crowds awed by the official placards : " Whoever applauds the King shall be thrashed, whoever insults him, hung." So Louis stayed on until the fatal 10th of August 1792, when the revolutionary mob stormed the palace and massacred the Swiss Guard, staunch mercenaries, true, as Carlyle says, to a king who was not their own. Three days afterwards the King and Queen and their children were in the Temple prison, and in the following May the Convention moved from the Salle de Manège, that stood in the Rue Castiglione on the other side of the Rue de Rivoli, to the Tuileries, destined to be for the next year or two the scene of the Revolutionary Government. But first Louis XVI. had been brought back to his palace to be tried and condemned.

In June 1794 the Tuileries gardens were packed with citizens and their families in holiday dress. Robespierre, " in sky-blue coat and black breeches," led the members of the Convention from their hall, with his own hand to light the pyre on which was a painted figure representing Atheism. It was the Fête of the Supreme Being, the new God of Robespierre's invention—a fatal innovation among a people so impatient of sentimentality and the unreal. " *Avec ton Être Suprême*," said one of his colleagues to Robespierre, " *tu commences à m'embêter*." Let it be recorded in slight mitigation of his many sins that it was Robespierre who ordered stone benches to be fixed in the Tuileries gardens on which the aged and the weary might rest.

Two years passed. Danton and Robespierre had followed the King and the Girondins into the unknown, and again the Paris crowd surged round the Tuileries. The Revolution had grown unpopular. The more prosperous Paris was vaguely royalist, and the Faubourgs, suspicious and resentful, surged west for the last time. The new men headed by Paul Barras, that clever scoundrel from Provence, were fearful for their places. A strong man was wanted, and the strong man was found. Bonaparte skilfully disposed his cannon. The Sectionnaires, most of them, so Napoleon declared, *Chouans de charette*, having been repulsed from the Tuileries, made their last stand on the steps of the Church of St. Roch before they were dispersed by the famous whiff of grape shot. " The thing we specifically call the French Revolution," says

RUE ST. HONORE—ST. ROCH.

Carlyle, "is blown into space by it and becomes a thing that was."

By November 1799 the Directory had run its course. Napoleon, now with the glory of a conqueror, backed by the army and aided by competent generals—Bernadotte alone hanging back—called together certain members of the Council of Ancients at the Tuileries at seven o'clock in the morning of November the 9th, the famous 18th Brumaire, and at three o'clock the next morning, the Consulate was proclaimed in the palace at St. Cloud. Two days afterwards Napoleon was living at the Luxembourg, where Bourrienne records that the word *Citoyenne* was dropped, and Josephine was addressed as Madame.

Less than six months afterwards Bonaparte removed to the Tuileries. Proceeding in a great procession with three thousand picked soldiers, and with his generals and his ministers, he entered the palace under the inscription, "Royalty is abolished in France and shall never be re-established." And in the entrance hall was a bust of Brutus, set there that no one should falsely suppose that Bonaparte hoped to be a king. The soldiers were reviewed in the gardens and, I quote Bourrienne, "a number of elegant females, dressed in the Grecian costume which was then the fashion, filled the windows." The inscription remained, and the bust, but the caps of liberty that had been painted on the walls were removed. "Wash all those things out," said Napoleon to the architect, "I won't have any such fooleries." In the morning, after his first night in a king's bedroom, he said: "Bourrienne, to be at the Tuileries is not all. We must remain here."

The day after Napoleon was proclaimed Emperor, he held the first Imperial levee at the Tuileries, the Parisians laughing loudly at the awkwardness of the new courtiers with their new high-sounding names. Pope Pius VII. had apartments in the Temple of Flora in the Tuileries when he came to Paris to crown Napoleon at Notre-Dame. "I must own that I never saw a man with a finer countenance or a more respectable appearance," said Rapp, the revolutionary soldier, who was to live to command a corps at Waterloo.

Saint Denis, Napoleon's valet de chambre, has left an interesting account of domestic life in the Tuileries after the marriage with Marie Louise and the birth of the King of Rome. It was the duty of Saint Denis to serve the Emperor at breakfast. He says:

"A few moments after His Majesty had sat down the Empress would appear. She would give her husband a kiss and sit down at his right. It was my duty to place a chair for her. Most frequently when the Emperor came out of his room he would be accompanied by some important person—a minister or some one—with whom he would continue his conversation till the Empress arrived, for when she was present all serious discussion was banished and playful chat took its place. At dessert the King of Rome was announced and Madame de Montesquiou, followed by an under-governess, would come in, carrying the young Prince in her arms. The Emperor would kiss his son and the talk would continue with the Empress, Madame de Montesquiou, and the person who was present.

"When breakfast was over the Emperor would take the little king in his arms and go to the window, to show him the people passing and a group of curious men and women who habitually stood under the window during breakfast. The little scenes of paternal love did not cease till the Emperor and Empress returned to the salon. . . .

"One day the Emperor took the little king in his arms after his breakfast, as was his custom, caressed him, played some little tricks on him, and said to the Empress, turning toward her, 'Here! kiss your son!' I do not remember now whether the Empress kissed the prince, but she replied in a tone almost of repugnance and disgust, 'I do not see how anybody can kiss a child.' The father was very different; he never stopped kissing and caressing his beloved son."

Poor little boy, for whom so much was planned and to whom so little was given!

After the battle of Leipzig, the prelude to the break-up of the Empire and Napoleon's banishment to Elba, Louis XVIII. took up his residence in the Tuileries Palace, but his stay was short. In March 1815 Napoleon landed in France, and great was the perturbation in Paris, councillors and ministers sitting all night discussing whether the King should flee, only Marmont, hard-bitten old marshal, suggesting that he should lock himself in the palace and stand a

RUE DE RIVOLI FROM THE TUILERIES

siege—a proceeding by no means to the stomach of the elderly Bourbon. On the night of the 20th March Napoleon was back in the Tuileries for the Hundred Days, and Louis was at Ghent. The second Restoration came, and with it the return to the palace of the King, who died there in 1834.

So the story goes on, revolution following revolution, poor Louis Philippe escaping in 1848 by an underground passage to his four-wheeled cab in the Place de la Concorde.

In 1853 Napoleon III. was installed at the Tuileries with his raffish Court. There was a smell of booty in the air, and the people who collected it were not of the nicest. It was in the Tuileries that Napoleon and Haussmann planned the rebuilding of Paris, and the rebuilding made the fortune of every inhabitant of the palace, from the great officers of State to the scullery maids, with the sole exception of Haussmann and the Emperor.

Life at the Tuileries during the Second Empire was exactly like an operette of Offenbach, with its chief characters the Emperor with his heavy moustache and constant cigarette, infinitely tolerant and infinitely bored, the Empress often sad and apprehensive, the Prince Imperial, born in the Tuileries, as the son of the first Napoleon had been, and fated for almost as tragic an end. The days saw a constant round of dances, private theatricals and *tableaux vivants*, with the Comte Tacher de la Pagerie, the Emperor's kinsman, supplying the comic relief with realistic imitations of barnyard fowls and barking dogs. All pure Offenbach. And Paris outside the Tuileries caught the note of the Court, with courtesans as popular heroines, laughing along the years, until Sedan and the Commune should bring it back to its senses.

It was on September 3, 1870, that the news came to Eugénie as she stood on the little staircase in the Tuileries reaching from her husband's study to her rooms, that Sedan was lost and Napoleon a prisoner. Outside the railings of the palace gardens the Paris crowd was chanting *Déchéance, Déchéance*. The next day Gambetta declared in the Chamber of Deputies that the dynasty had ceased to reign and, that afternoon, Eugénie slipped away by the gallery that led from the Tuileries to the Louvre, out into the Rue de Rivoli, where she took a closed cab to the house of an American dentist. As she drove along the street she saw workmen already busy taking down the Imperial eagles. "*Déjà*," was her bitter comment.

Paris was sore and humiliated, and the bitterness increased when the conquering Germans marched through the Arc de Triomphe, to bivouac on the Place de la Concorde. Paris was indeed very angry. She felt she had been betrayed. She had been the victim of the Emperor. She was now the victim of Gambetta and Thiers. The provinces were indifferent to her sufferings, but Paris was still Paris, she would govern herself. The Faubourgs should rise again. There should be another revolution. So menacing were the people that M. Thiers, the President of the new Republic, and his ministers withdrew from Paris to Versailles, and another siege began, this time Frenchmen fighting against Frenchmen.

There was enthusiasm enough in the ranks of the Communists, but their leaders were inept, and their General Cluseret was a super-incompetent. "It was this military pamphlet-maker," says the Communist historian, Lissagaray, "with no pledge but his decoration won against the Socialists in 1848, who had played the marionette in three insurrections, whom the Socialists in 1871 charged with the defence of their revolution." It was a pitiful business, hopeless from the beginning, but only brought to an end after bitter and often heroic struggles.

The oddest and most futile of the Communards was Paul Verlaine, the poet. Verlaine had married the eminently respectable, rather dull Mathilde Mautet, in the summer of 1870. He was neither a brave man nor in any sense a patriot, and when he was told that the Germans might enter Paris, he merely remarked: "Well, at least we shall have some good music." When the siege actually began he was compelled to enlist in the National Guard, but he spent most of his time on the fortifications getting drunk with his comrades. So badly indeed did he behave that his young wife left him and returned to her parents. Although he knew nothing of politics, Verlaine had many Bohemian friends among the Communards, and their revolt against respectability and the *bourgeoisie* struck him as an amusing adventure. He had been before in the Government service, and he returned to his old employment, acting as censor of the press and dealing drastically with the

THE PLAÇE JEANNE D'ARC, RUE DE RIVOLI

anti-revolutionist papers. How little or how much he actually had to do with the Commune no one really knows. He used to say that he and he alone saved Notre-Dame from destruction, but that probably was a mere boast. Anyhow, when the end came, Verlaine was in a state of terror, hiding himself in his wife's parents' flat and eventually succeeding in escaping from Paris.

The adventure was a mock-heroic episode in the life of a poet, sadder perhaps than that of any other poet except his countryman, François Villon. All Paris mourned when Paul Verlaine died in 1896, and five thousand people stood around his grave with its pall of orchids and lilac in the cemetery of Batignolles ; but Mr. Nicholson has well said that the homage was " an apology, almost an expiation to a great writer who had been neglected and unappreciated, the tragedy being that it was impossible for a person with his qualities not to be neglected and unappreciated." Genius is not necessarily respectable. Verlaine was a drunkard, a drug maniac, and worse. But he was one of the greatest of the French poets. Anatole France has said : " *Certes il est fou. Mais prenez garde que ce pauvre insensé a créé un art nouveau et qu'il y a quelque chance qu'on dise un jour : ' c'était le meilleur poète de son temps.'* "

Verlaine was a great sinner, and, like many another great sinner, he " got religion." The conversion was not enduring, but Anatole France was convinced of its sincerity. " As sincere in sin as in repentance, he accepted the alternatives with cynical innocence," and he has written some of the finest Christian poetry in the French language ; witness the poem that begins :

O mon Dieu, vous m'avez blessé d'amour
Et la blessure est encore vibrante ;
O mon Dieu, vous m'avez blessé d'amour.

Voici mon front qui n'a pu que rougir,
Pour l'escabeau de vos pieds adorables,
Voici mon front qui n'a pu que rougir.

Voici mes mains qui n'ont pas travaillé
Pour les charbons ardents et l'encens rare,
Voici mes mains qui n'ont point travaillé.

To return to the Commune, the Government troops from Versailles invaded Paris on the morning of May 25,

1871, and barricade fighting took place all through the day. First Montmartre was captured, and the troops fought their way down the hill. There was a pitched battle in the Rue Haussmann, near the great Printemps stores. There was fighting in the Faubourg St. Honoré, and blazing houses in the Rue Royale. The Place de la Concorde was a shambles. The Place Vendôme was captured, and there was fighting in the Rue de Rivoli, and at nightfall the Tuileries Palace was ablaze. The building that has recalled so many moving historical events, which Catherine de Médicis built, where Louis XVI. suffered, and where the two Napoleons had their few years of glory, was completely destroyed. Perhaps the ghost of the little Dauphin watched the burning walls of a palace which had been his childhood's prison, and, may be, the little sad ghost smiled a little as he watched.

THE HUGUENOT CHURCH, RUE DE RIVOLI

IV

THE LOUVRE

THE Louvre is the most famous building in the world. If the Tower, Windsor Castle, Kensington Palace and the National Gallery were all in one immense block, London would possess a building with some, but by no means all, the historical interest of the Palais du Louvre in Paris. *Le vrai Palais de la France, tout le monde l'a nommé, c'est le Louvre.* The origin of the name is uncertain. There is a fantastic suggestion that it is derived from *lupus*, a wolf, since the first Louvre was built outside the walls of Paris and was sometimes used as a royal hunting-box. There is another suggestion that the word comes from *louver*, a blockhouse, for the old Louvre had a tower that commanded the Seine, as the Tower of London commands the Thames.

The Palais du Louvre was first built in the twelfth century by King Philippe II., sometimes known as Philippe-Auguste, whom we English remember because of his quarrel with Richard Cœur de Lion when they went together on Crusade. A shrewd man was Philippe, " of agreeable face and ruddy complexion, loving good cheer, wine and women." It was he who laid the foundations of the French absolute monarchy, cultivating good relations with the middle class, beginning the long struggle between the King and the great princes, and steadily befriending the Church, though this did not save him from very proper excommunication when he proposed to repudiate an uncomely Danish princess whom he had married for reasons of State. It was after his return from the Holy Land, having lost his hair at the siege of Acre, that Philippe began building the Louvre with its four towers and a central keep. It was a simple enough building, used in its early days more often as a prison than a palace.

It was in the Louvre that the peers were called together to condemn King John of England for the murder of Prince Arthur and to deprive him of his fiefs in France, proceedings which greatly added to the power and influence of the French King. Philippe's grandson, St. Louis—saint, scholar and most efficient king—lived in the old palace of the kings that stood in the *cité* near Notre-Dame. There he fed the poor and humble, there he fasted and prayed, and there he entertained such guests as St. Thomas Aquinas, whom he loved to honour. But it was in the Louvre that St. Louis once gave a dramatic demonstration of his love of justice. One Enguerrand of Coucy, had hanged three boys who had trespassed on his land, shooting at his rabbits with bow and arrow. Justice was demanded, as usual, by the Church, and Enguerrand was arrested and imprisoned in the Louvre. He was tried by his peers, the majority deeply resenting the suggestion that a great lord might not hang a poacher. But Louis was insistent and Enguerrand was condemned to a heavy fine for the endowment of masses for the souls of his victims, and to lose certain of his rights. This affair, says a chronicler, was a great example of justice to other kings, seeing that a man of such noble lineage, accused by poor and simple folk, barely escaped with his life before the lover and upholder of right.

St. Louis stands alone among the kings of Europe. Our own Edward is a saint and, so it is said, our Henry VI. is soon to be canonised, but neither Edward nor Henry was very wise, while Louis was both wise and good. " Many men wondered," says the chronicler after the great King's death, " that one man so meek, so gentle, not strong of body nor strenuous in labour, could reign peacefully over so great a kingdom and so many powerful lords, especially as he was neither lavish in presence nor very complacent to some of them." By his achievements, St. Louis demonstrated that when on a rare occasion the meek inherit the earth, they are able to administer it admirably. The children of light are, happily, more than a match for the children of this world.

Charles V. extended the Louvre, building twelve new towers, in one of which he began the French National

THE LOUVRE

Library. Stormy meetings of the *États Généraux*, the mediæval parliament of France, were held in the Louvre, while Charles's father was a prisoner in England after the defeat at Poitiers. The Paris merchants, backed by the Church, demanded the dismissal of certain royal ministers. They had already conceived the idea of no taxation without representation. The history of the French States-General is very different from that of the English Parliament. They went on meeting regularly through the fourteenth and fifteenth centuries, but the French kings, unlike the English, succeeded in establishing absolutism, and with the beginning of the Bourbon period, the influence of the States-General came to an end. They met once after the accession of Henri IV.—and then not again till 1789.

The Louvre must have been a pleasant place in the time of Charles V. who, in his private life, attempted to follow in the footsteps of St. Louis. He laid out the Louvre gardens, planting the beds with strawberries and hyssop, and sage and lavender. The first clocks ever seen in France were installed in his palace, and in the records of his expenditure there is a payment of twenty francs to the servant "who guards our nightingales of our chastel of the Louvre."

Louis XI., the ablest of the Valois (the king immortalised in *Quentin Durward*), cared little for the Louvre. He had a complete contempt for all palaces and all the trappings of royalty.

The next king concerned with the extension of the palace was François I., the prince of the Renaissance who met Henry VIII. on the Field of the Cloth of Gold, and was his rival as patron of the new learning. François brought Benvenuto Cellini from Italy to Paris and lodged him in the Tour de Nesle, that he might suggest embellishments to the Louvre. But it was pulling down rather than building with which François was concerned. He was an attractive democratic king, the friend of poets and artists—Ronsard's father was his *maître d'hôtel*—greatly beloved by his daughter-in-law, Catherine de Médicis, when she arrived at the French Court, very young and very timid. "All is lost save honour," François is said to have exclaimed when the defeat at Pavia brought his blundering Italian campaign to an end. It is sad to be obliged to add that he was by no means so epigrammatic. He actually wrote to his mother :

"Of all things nothing remains to me but honour and life, which is safe."

The Louvre was the scene of the tragedy of St. Bartholomew. Charles IX. was the second son of Catherine de Médicis to be King of France, and despite St. Bartholomew's Eve the only one of her sons who excites pity and not contempt. He was a puny man, with a crooked neck and a prematurely wrinkled face, but he had notably beautiful eyes. He had none of the vices of his brothers. He was a sensitive, impressionable, melancholy man of good intentions. He loved music and poetry, and Ronsard was his friend.

Ronsard was essentially a Court poet. It is to the credit of the later Valois—there is not too much to their credit—that they appreciated and encouraged the genius of the seven stars of the *Pléïade*, the poets of whom Ronsard was by far the greatest, who set out to make French poetry as great as that of Greece and Rome. Ronsard was the first modern French poet. He was essentially national in imagination and expression, and kings and princes made life easy for him. He had apartments at the Louvre. He received a handsome income from many abbeys and priories. And it is curious that in an age of murder and sudden death, and in a palace atmosphere teeming with intrigue—it seems probable that Ronsard was at the Louvre on the eve of St. Bartholomew—he should have written such delicious poetry as his :

Mignonne, allons voir si la Rose,
Qui ce matin avait desclose
    Sa robe de pourpre au soleil,
A point perdu cette vesprée
Les plis de sa robe pourprée
    Et son teint au vostre pareil.

Las ! voyez comme en peu d'espace,
Mignonne, elle a dessus la place,
    Las, las, ses beautez laissé cheoir !
O vraiment marâtre Nature,
Puisqu'une telle fleur ne dure
    Que du matin jusques au soir.

Donc, si vous me croyez, Mignonne,
Tandis que votre âge fleuronne
    En sa plus verte nouveauté,
Cueillez, cueillez votre jeunesse ;
Comme à cette fleur, la vieillesse
    Fera ternir votre beauté.

THE HOTEL BRETONVILLIERS, ILE ST. LOUIS

Charles, the friend of Ronsard and himself, as Mr. Saintsbury testifies, no bad poet, sanctioned the massacre of St. Bartholomew, for Charles the Well Intentioned was also Charles the Mad. Generally he was quiet, orderly and domestic, carefully making entries in his account books that supply interesting details of everyday life in the Louvre in the sixteenth century, as, for example: "Ten livres for washing the pages' heads and sponging their hair." But often he suffered from fits of insane frenzy, and he lived in terrified subjection to his mother, now grown very fat but still a "great eater of all things indifferently."

In September 1571 the great Admiral Coligny, the leader of the Huguenots, arrived at the Louvre. The young King loved the old man. He talked to him of a France with great colonial possessions filched from the Spanish in South America. He told him of a plan for incorporating half the Protestant Netherlands into the Valois kingdom. The King was fascinated. And Catherine grew jealous, the Guises, always a turbulent family, feeling political power slipping from them, grew apprehensive, and Paris, that had no love for Protestants, grew angry. Coligny talked, and Catherine sat in her apartments in the Louvre, waiting and plotting. She was no religious fanatic. Like Elizabeth she used religions as political pawns in the game of maintaining personal power. That was her one and constant end. At this time she was eager to marry her daughter, Marguerite, to Henri of Navarre, and she was entirely unaffected by the fact that Marguerite sulked and wept, and that her love for the handsome Henri de Guise was notorious to the whole Court. Protestant Navarre must be joined to Catholic France in order to make the Spanish frontier safe. Henri's mother, the stern Puritan, Jeanne d'Albret, came to Paris much against her will—a wonderful lady, pious, intellectual, uncomfortably outspoken. She arrived in May, and died in June. The Louvre was an unhealthy place in the days of Catherine de Médicis, but there seems no reason to suppose that Queen Jeanne was murdered.

The massacre of St. Bartholomew was the result of religious fanaticism, deliberately inflamed for political purposes. Catherine, probably wisely, was opposed to Coligny's policy of an alliance with the Prince of Orange against Spain, and it seemed to her that the best way to deal with a political enemy was to kill him. The Huguenots, too, a small well-to-do, lawless community, were a constant source of difficulty and trouble. " Every northern pirate," says Miss Sichel, " could call himself a Protestant and find a home in all-embracing La Rochelle." Moreover, Catherine realised that if the Huguenots were not broken, a cruel war between Coligny and the Guises would bring misery to France and would seriously weaken the power of the throne. So the massacre was planned.

Meanwhile, Paris was filling for the marriage of Marguerite and Henri, Huguenots and followers of the Duc de Guise pouring into the city, while shopkeepers shut up their shops, and sober citizens anticipated trouble. The marriage took place on August 18, 1572, Marguerite kneeling at the nuptial mass in Notre-Dame while her Protestant husband paced up and down with Coligny in the courtyard. On the 22nd, Coligny was fired at and wounded. King Charles was furiously indignant, and the Huguenots, believing in his power to protect them, grew more confident and assured. Then in the streets of Paris and in the passages of the Louvre there were whispers of a great Protestant conspiracy against the lives of the Queen Mother and her sons. There was probably little enough in these rumours, but they served Catherine's purpose. She reported the rumours to the King, assuring him that his life was in danger, that Coligny was a traitor, that he must either kill the Protestants or they would kill him, and at last she had her way. The kindly King disappeared, and the mad King appeared with foam on his mouth shouting, " You have willed it, well then, kill them all, kill them all ! "

Catherine had prepared and she quietly awaited events at the hour of her *coucher*, with her two daughters sitting together on a coffer, pale-faced and terrified, and occasionally bursting into tears—and then the bells of St. Germain l'Auxerrois sounded, and the massacre began. Two thousand Huguenots, Coligny among them, were done to death, a fearful enough total, but a small thing indeed compared to the massacres of Christians that have taken place in Russia and Asia Minor since the War, and against which western Europe has hardly made a protest. From

STEAMBOAT PIER, HOTEL DE VILLE

the windows of the Louvre the Queen Mother and her ladies watched the killing with eager interest, but the Queen, a gentle pious Catholic, knelt in prayer for her husband who had been compelled into crime : " My God, I entreat, I demand of Thee that Thou wilt mercifully forgive him, for if Thou hast not pity upon him I fear that this sin will be pardoned by none else ! "

Charles died three years after the massacre. His last words were : " I rejoice that I leave no male child to wear the crown after me."

The bells of St. Germain l'Auxerrois which gave the signal for the beginning of the St. Bartholomew killing were always tolled at royal funerals. They are still the finest bells in the city. St. Germain of Auxerrois was a Burgundian prince who, " realising his vocation, gave all his riches to the poor people and changed his wife into his sister," thereafter performing many miracles and attaining a great reputation for his saintliness. The church began as a small oratory, built in the sixth century, and it became the church to which the citizens of Paris generally sent their children for baptism. In the time of Charlemagne a school grew up in connection with the church which gave its name to the adjacent Rue de l'École. Most of the present church belongs to the fourteenth and fifteenth centuries, marred by the vandalism of the later eighteenth century.

Its proximity to the Louvre and the Tuileries made St. Germain l'Auxerrois with St. Roch the churches of the French kings and queens. Marie Antoinette went regularly to mass at St. Germain's, where her *prie-dieu* may still be seen, and it was a priest from the church, " a constitutional priest in lay dress," who was with her, " a wan, discrowned widow of thirty-eight," when she was taken from the Palais de Justice to the Place de la Révolution.

In the short-lived atheistic frenzy of the Revolution, St. Germain's lost much of its old stained glass, some of which, however, remains to show how much more beautiful ancient glass is than modern. During the revolutionary troubles that drove the Bourbons from France and made Louis Philippe the Citizen King, the church was attacked by a mob who did considerable damage, despite Victor Hugo's assurance that " *la population de Paris s'est admirablement conduite pendant le combat et après la victoire*." The statue of the Virgin was discovered undamaged among the débris. It now stands in the well-named Chapelle Notre Dame de Bonne Garde.

The Louvre was the scene of almost inconceivable follies after the death of Charles IX. and during the reign of Henri III.—a coward and a poltroon, fond of nursing lap-dogs, who blazoned death's-heads all over his clothes and on his shoe-strings in sign of mourning for his mistress. One evening the King gave a banquet at which all the guests, dressed in green, were waited on by ladies in men's clothes of the same colour. This cost him sixty thousand francs. On another night a number of Italians won thirty thousand crowns off him at play. The King lodged alchemists in the palace and then, as an antidote, read himself to sleep every night with Machiavelli's *The Prince*.

Among the many tasks to which the vigorous Henri of Navarre set his hand was the rebuilding of Paris, which, during the Valois era, was little more than "a sea of squalid houses round a few isolated palaces or churches of superb architecture." He added greatly to the Louvre, building the gallery which joined the palace to the Tuileries, which had then only just been completed. He was a great man and a gallant. "When I am gone," he said shortly before his death, "you will know what you have lost," and after his assassination by Ravaillac in 1610, France indeed discovered that she had lost a King.

Richelieu, in so many ways the heir of Henri IV., was another great builder, and he too added to the Louvre before building his own Palais-Cardinal. It was in the Louvre that the great Cardinal intrigued against Anne of Austria. It was in the Louvre that d'Artagnan and the three musketeers were received by Louis XIII. "When M. d'Artagnan is on duty he is to be found at the Louvre." It was the Louvre that until the accession of Louis XIV. was the home of the French kings and the scene of persistent picturesque intrigues. Colbert, the minister of Louis XIV., who invented protective tariffs, carried on the grandiose plans of Henri IV. and Richelieu, but at his death the Louvre ceased to be a royal residence. Louis XIV. hated living in Paris and built the palace of Versailles which, as Mr. Belloc says somewhere, was destined to be the grave-yard of the French monarchy. In 1670, 1,627,293 livres

THE ILE DE LA CITE

were spent on the Louvre. In 1680 the subsidy had entirely ceased, and it was not until 1754 that anything further was done to the great building which, during the interregnum had become a sort of glorified lodging-house, its inmates including the hangers-on of the Court, poor artists, and defaulting debtors. A king of Denmark who visited the Louvre in 1678 has left an epigrammatic description of the palace :

> J'ai vu le Louvre et son enceinte immense,
> Vaste palais qui depuis deux cent ans
> Toujours s'achève et toujours se commence.
> Deux ouvriers, manœuvres fainéants,
> Hâtent très lentement ces riches bâtiments
> Et sont payés, quand on y pense.

On October 24, 1658, Molière and his company gave a performance of Corneille's tragedy *Nicomède* at the Louvre before Louis XIV. and his Court. Molière had started his career as a theatrical manager fourteen years before with a Paris season that had been an entire failure. For twelve years he had been touring the provinces, going from town to town on horseback or on foot, wandering all over France, making influential friends like the Prince de Conti, saving money and establishing a considerable reputation. It was through the King's brother that the performance was given at the Louvre " to the Queen Mother and to the King." After the performance Molière, a stately, attractive figure with large mouth, full lips, swarthy complexion and bushy eyebrows, addressed the King in well-turned phrases, and captured the heart of the audience, which included the great Mazarin. So complete was the conquest that the Petit Bourbon, which communicated with the Louvre by a gallery, was put at his disposal, and there he produced his *L'Étourdi*, and in the autumn of 1659 *Les Précieuses Ridicules*. Molière stayed in the Louvre until the Petit Bourbon was pulled down, when his company moved over to the Palais-Royal.

In 1662 Molière, then a man of forty, was married at the Louvre's church, St. Germain l'Auxerrois, to Armande Béjard, a girl of nineteen. The marriage was not a success. Armande was a brilliant woman with a cold, hard temperament, the original of Célimène in her husband's great comedy, *Le Misanthrope*.

After the Revolution the National Convention decided that the Louvre should become the National Museum. In 1794 the Petite Galerie was used as a bourse. The artistic treasures filched by Napoleon during his campaign in Italy were installed by the Directory in the galleries of the Louvre, and in 1802, when he was First Consul, Napoleon, anticipating the Prince Consort, held an industrial exhibition there. Ten years later, such is the irony of history, special apartments were prepared in the Louvre for the entertainment of the foreign sovereigns who were expected to come to Paris after the successful termination of the campaign in Russia.

Nowadays the palace of Dumas and the Valois houses the finest collection of pictures in northern Europe—" Monna Lisa " (La Joconde), with the mystic smile, masterpieces of Raphael, Titian, Velasquez, Veronese, Botticelli, Murillo, Rembrandt, Van Dyck, and all the great masters. It was François I. who began the collection by buying, while he was in Italy, " Monna Lisa " from Leonardo da Vinci for a sum which in our money would be twenty thousand pounds.

V

THE PALAIS-ROYAL

NOWADAYS the gardens of the Palais-Royal are generally deserted and not a little depressing. They suggest the used-to-be though they provide a restful relief from the crowds and the noise of the streets round the Magasins du Louvre. In 1629 Richelieu bought the site occupied by the Hôtel de Mercœur and the Hôtel Rambouillet in the neighbourhood of the Louvre and commenced the building of the Palais-Cardinal which from his death has been known as the Palais-Royal. In the first half of the seventeenth century the Hôtel Rambouillet had been the meeting-place of aristocrats and men of letters, much in the same way as Holland House was in England at the beginning of the nineteenth century.

It was from the Palais-Cardinal that Richelieu ruled France, sleeping little, working with indomitable energy, and finding occasionally relaxation in the private performance of plays and ballets. Corneille's *Cid* was acted twice in Richelieu's palace, and for a time the poet was attached to his household. The Cardinal was always eager to play Maecenas to the literary men of his age, a noble army that included Molière, Pascal and Descartes, and it was in the Palais-Cardinal that the French Academy was founded.

Thanks mainly to Dumas, Richelieu has become one of the villains of historical melodrama. He is remembered as the employer of Miladi, and the enemy of d'Artagnan, and to be the foe of that matchless hero is naturally and properly to be numbered with the infamous. But the real Richelieu, as Dumas himself thoroughly realised, was a very great man and no more a villain than great men, when they are unchecked, are apt to be. There is a contemporary description of him in the *Memoirs* of Cardinal de Retz :

" Richelieu was a man who kept his word whenever no great interest forced him to do otherwise, and in that case he neglected nothing that was calculated to save his appearance of good faith. He was not liberal, but he gave more than he promised, and his way of adding zest to the benefits he conferred was admirable. He cared for glory far more than morality permits ; but it must be acknowledged that his abuse of the dispensation he had granted himself touching the excess of his ambition was no greater than his merit warranted. . . . He was a good friend ; he would even have desired the love of the people : but though he possessed the civility, the appearance, and many other qualities necessary to this result, he never had that indescribable something which is more indispensable in this matter than in any other. . . . No man could distinguish better than he between bad and worse, between good and better, and that is a very great quality in a minister. He was too apt to grow impatient over the small things that lead up to the great ; but this fault, which is peculiar to lofty minds, is always accompanied by a sagacity which makes amends for it. He had sufficient religion for the purposes of this world. He inclined towards that which is good, whether by preference or by good sense, whenever his interests did not lead him towards evil, which he recognised perfectly well, even when he did it. . . . To conclude, it must be acknowledged that all his vices were of a kind which a high fortune easily renders illustrious, for they were of those which can only use great virtues as their instruments."

Richelieu loved luxury and was vulgarly ostentatious. He was proud and often insolent. He was a shameless nepotist. He was incapable of pity and he had no friends. He was nearly always ill, suffering agonies from headaches and subject to half a dozen chronic complaints, but his will was unbreakable and his energy tireless. A fierce assured figure of a man of whom even d'Artagnan was reasonably afraid—and a great servant of France.

Since the well-being of a nation depends on the creation of an all-powerful central authority, in finally establishing the unchallengeable authority of the sovereign, Richelieu

THE PALAIS ROYAL

was serving his country as well as serving his king. He finished the task that Louis XI. had begun and that Catherine de Médicis, in face of infinite difficulties, and Henri IV. and Sully had continued. The power of the feudal princes and nobles and of the Huguenots had to be destroyed before France could be assured of internal peace. That was Richelieu's achievement, and it was not calculated to make him popular in his own time. In foreign affairs his policy was to make France dominant in Europe by humbling the Hapsburgs, and in this Louis XIV. reaped where he had sowed.

The relations between Louis XIII. and his great minister have been often discussed. Louis was a sickly man who, nevertheless, managed to live to middle age despite the ruthless energy of his doctors who, in one year, bled him fifty-seven times, dosed him with two hundred and twelve purgatives and gave him two hundred and fifteen injections! He was modest, fastidious and self-distrustful, a sad sombrely clothed man in a gay Court. He was in appearance a typical Bourbon, with the family characteristics exaggerated to the point of caricature. The large Bourbon nose was far too large. The under lip was almost grotesquely pendulous. His head was too big and his legs pitifully thin. But Louis was no fool. He never forgot that he was the son of Henri IV., and in a very real sense he was King of France. He listened to Richelieu. But he decided for himself, and not always in accord with the Cardinal's wishes. As M. Jacques Boulenger says:

"It was never either feebleness or indolence that led Louis XIII. to follow the counsels of his great minister. He followed them because he was too sensible not to recognise the Cardinal's superior gifts, and that being so, too honest not to submit to them."

This is not, I fear, the Louis of *Les Trois Mousquetaires*, but it is the Louis of history.

In his will Richelieu left the Palais-Cardinal to Louis XIII., "the intention of the Cardinal being that it will serve as a residence for his Majesty and his successors or for heirs of the Crown, having built this palace at such expense with that design." The King only lived for a few months after his great minister, and at his death, Anne of Austria, who became Regent for her son Louis XIV., moved from the uncomfortable Louvre to the new palace, fitted, as the house agents would say, with all modern conveniences.

Anne of Austria has been made familiar by the romances of Alexandre Dumas. When she took up her residence at the Palais-Royal she was a good-looking, healthy woman of forty-two, very devout, even-tempered, with moments of petulant passion, and, despite Dumas, virtuous and scrupulous. Like most of the men and women of her time Anne had a prodigious appetite. Louis XIV. regularly ate through an appalling menu, and this capacity was inherited from his mother. " She always breakfasted before she heard mass. She was served after her broth with cutlets, sausages and bread porridge. She generally ate a little of everything and did not dine the less heartily."

They were happy days for Anne when she first moved to the Palais-Royal. Richelieu was dead, the Queen's goodness was everywhere acclaimed, and Mazarin, the new Prime Minister, the smooth Sicilian to whom the Queen had given apartments in the Palace, " so as to be able to confer with him on her business more conveniently," was not yet unpopular. His strength, it was said, " lay in soft words, hinting, giving reason to hope." But Anne's peace was short-lived. The war with Spain was successful enough but costly, and the people, in the common manner of the French, clamoured loudly against the necessary taxes. Women threw themselves at the Queen's feet when she went to Notre-Dame, warning her that " she had a man about her who took everything." The Cardinal became unpopular at Court because he prevented corruption, and the fantastic conspiracy of the Fronde began, peers and great ladies conspiring with the Parliament, that resented the loss of its privileges, and the people who hated paying their taxes.

Alexandre Dumas has nothing but scorn for Mazarin. He describes him as " that mean fellow who tries to put on his head a crown which he has stolen under a pillow ; that puppy who calls his party that of the king, and who bethought himself of putting the princes of the blood into prison, not daring to kill them, as did the great cardinal ; a skinflint who weighs his golden crowns and keeps the clipped ones from fear that although he cheats he may lose them at his next day's game."

THE FLOWER MARKET

Angry scenes took place in the Palais-Royal after Mazarin had ordered the arrest of two of the Paris councillors who had been particularly outspoken in their criticisms. Paris is always terrifying when she grows angry, and prudence dictated the flight of the Queen Mother, the King and Mazarin from the Palace, on Twelfth Night, 1649. The child King and his little brother were taken out of their beds at three in the morning and driven through the darkness to St. Germain-en-Laye. But Paris, ever fickle, grew tired of the Frondeurs and Frondeuses—of the posing of great ladies like Mme. de Longueville, always imitating the heroines of romance, and protesting, " I do not care for innocent pleasures "—and by August, Anne was back again in the Palais-Royal, arriving amidst a scene of great popular enthusiasm. The new mood passed and troubles began again, fomented by the truculent Cardinal de Retz, of whom it was said : " His whole life from one end to the other was ruled by his will. His immorality was sublime and his greatness of soul never failed him." There was indeed no tranquillity for Anne until Louis XIV. attained his majority and the Regency came to an end. " At her son's Court," says M. Jacques Boulenger, " Anne's one great aim was to play the part of an old lady tastefully, and right well did she succeed."

In 1652 the King took up his residence in the Louvre, and this meant that Queen Henrietta Maria, widow of Charles I., had to move from the Louvre, where she had been given shelter after her escape from England, to the Palais-Royal. She and her children had suffered not a little from France's civil troubles. Cardinal de Retz records that they had been left without a faggot for a fire and that the Queen had been obliged to keep her daughter in bed because of the cold. Charles was with his mother when she was established at the Palais-Royal, and with him was Wilmot, afterwards the Earl of Rochester, already his evil influence, ready to make trouble between mother and son. But before many months France recognised the government of Cromwell, and the next year Charles went back to Holland. Henrietta Maria, mourning her dead husband and woefully disappointed in her son, remained at the Palais-Royal until the Restoration and until after the marriage of her daughter with the Duc d'Orléans, the King's brother.

It was on March 31, 1661, that Henriette Anne, the only daughter of Charles I. and Henrietta Maria, was married in the chapel of the Palais-Royal to Philippe d'Orléans, brother of Louis XIV. Henriette Anne was sixteen, charming, gentle, deliciously attractive. It was said of her: "When she speaks to you she seems to ask for your heart at once." Philippe d'Orléans was a hopeless decadent, "as foppish as two or three women." He minced and simpered and painted his face, was beringed and curled and indolent, and was always attended by favourites as offensive as himself. Louis XIV. was himself greatly attracted by his charming sister-in-law, and it was in order to prevent scandalous talk at Court that he began the intrigue with Louise de la Vallière, who was one of Henriette's maids of honour, and with whom he had the most idyllic of his love affairs. Henriette's daughter was born at the Palais-Royal in 1662, and eight years afterwards, after a visit to England in which she had negotiated the disgraceful Treaty by which her brother sold his country to the French, she died suddenly at St. Cloud after drinking a glass of chicory water. It was suspected that she was poisoned by one of her husband's favourites whom she had caused to be banished, but she actually died of peritonitis.

The year after her death there was another mistress at the Palais-Royal. The Duc d'Orléans' second wife, Elizabeth Charlotte, daughter of the Elector Palatine, was a very ugly lady who must have had an immense sense of humour, since she has left us a candid portrait of herself: "My figure is monstrously fat; I am as square as a cube; my skin is red with yellow patches on it; my hair is getting quite grey; my nose and my two cheeks as well have been horribly scarred by smallpox; I have a large mouth and bad teeth, and there you have a portrait of my pretty face." Elizabeth Charlotte had no accomplishments. French cooking turned her honest German stomach, and she spent her days abusing Mme. de Maintenon as an old horror, and longing for a good dish of sauerkraut with smoked sausages. That she was not without intelligence is shown by her remark concerning her august brother-in-law: "The King imagines he is pious when every one else is bored." She was deeply attached to her son, afterwards the notorious Regent,

SEINE QUAYSIDE

and was furiously angry when, at his uncle's order, he agreed to marry Mlle. de Blois, the daughter of Louise de la Vallière. The morning after he had given the promise, when her son approached his mother, " Madame gave him such a sounding box on the ears that it was heard some paces off, covering the poor Prince with confusion in the presence of the whole Court, and filling the numerous spectators with prodigious amazement."

Philippe d'Orléans died in 1701, and the Palais-Royal passed to his son, who became Regent of France after the death of Louis XIV., and until Louis XV. attained his majority. The Regent is an historical enigma. Saint-Simon, who had sincere affection for him, confesses that he never understood him. He was a man of inconsistence and contradiction, in many respects, as it seems to me, resembling Louis Napoleon. When Louis XIV. died he was the only legitimate prince of adult age and, as the King's nephew, the obvious regent during the childhood of Louis XV. But Louis XIV. mistrusted him and Mme. de Maintenon hated him. D'Orléans had great parts. He had proved himself a gallant soldier. He was generous, courteous and exceedingly intelligent. But his debaucheries were notorious and were particularly offensive in the Puritan atmosphere of de Maintenon's Versailles, and his liberal sympathies made it probable that if he became Regent he would insist on toleration for the Protestants. Louis XIV., therefore, on the advice of his wife, provided in his will for a Council of Regency of which d'Orléans should only be one member, but at the King's death the Duc applied to the Parliament of Paris and he became sole Regent, as was his right.

Politically he succeeded—and failed. He stopped religious persecution. He cut down further expenditure, but he countenanced John Law's financial schemes which ended in disaster. By his alliance with England and Holland he ensured peace at least for a season. All this is forgotten, while the orgies of the Palais-Royal of which the Regent was the central figure with Dubois as his chief minister and pander, are remembered. Dubois was an astute politician and a most evil man. Saint-Simon, who hated him, says :

" He was a little, pitiful, wizened, herring-gutted man,

in a flaxen wig, with a weasel's face, brightened by some intellect. All the vices—perfidy, avarice, debauchery, ambition, flattery—fought within him for the mastery. He was so consummate a liar that, when taken in the fact, he could brazenly deny it. Even his wit and knowledge of the world were spoiled, and his affected gaiety was touched with sadness by the odour of falsehood which escaped through every pore of his body."

The cynicism of d'Orléans—and again I think of Louis Napoleon—was shown when he made Dubois Archbishop of Cambrai, although he was married and not in holy orders. One of his courtiers protested: "What! That man Archbishop of Cambrai! Why, you told me yourself that he was a miserable, worthless, unbelieving dog." "So he is," said the Regent, "and that's just the reason why I have made the appointment; when he's an archbishop he will have to go to communion."

The principal political event of the Regency was the conspiracy to supplant d'Orléans by Philip V. of Spain, the grandson of Louis XIV., a morose sovereign who had to be kept under lock and key by his masterful Italian wife to prevent him from abdicating. D'Orléans showed characteristic mercy to the conspirators, whom he never seems to have taken very seriously. In the quarrels between France and Spain during the Regency, Dubois had as an opponent another strange churchman, Cardinal Alberoni, who began life as a bell-ringer and owed his first advancement to his skill in making *soupe au fromage*.

The Palais-Royal remained in the Orléans family until the Revolution. Philippe's son, Louis, was a harmless person who spent most of his time translating the Psalms and the Epistles of St. Paul into French. Carlyle tells us that he honestly believed that there was no death. On one occasion he was vastly indignant with his secretary who used the phrase *feu roi d'Espagne*. His son, Louis Philippe, fought at Fontenoy, and is remembered for nothing much else than that he was the father of the Philippe Égalité of the Revolution, and the grandfather of Louis Philippe, the Citizen King, who lost his throne because he preferred an umbrella to a sceptre. Philippe Égalité inherited the Palais-Royal in 1785, but during his father's lifetime he had built three large galleries which

LES BAINS ANCIENS

still surround the palace, letting them out in shops, so that the Palais became *un bazar européen et un rendez-vous d'affaires et des galanteries.* Two years before the Revolution he built and opened the Théâtre du Palais-Royal which, when I was a youth, was famous for the production of farces, the one constant quality of which was their impropriety. Carlyle declares that Philippe Égalité made of the Palais-Royal "the sorcerer's Sabbath and Satan-at-home of our planet."

Among the buildings of the Palais-Royal was the Café de Foy, before which, on July 12, 1789, Camille Desmoulins, for once losing his stammer, delivered to the people of Paris the great speech that really began the Revolution: "*Citoyens, j'arrive de Versailles,* the time for talking has gone, the time for action has come. The people must take up arms, they must show by their cockades to which party they are pledged. *Quelle couleur voulez-vous?*" The next day the Bastille fell. To-day there is a statue of Camille in the dull, quiet Palais-Royal gardens.

After the Revolution the Palais-Royal became Le Palais et Jardins de la Révolution. Napoleon established the Tribune in the Palace, and then at the beginning of a commercial century it became the home of the Bourse de Commerce. Lucien Bonaparte, the one of Napoleon's brothers who refused to be a king and spent the days of Napoleonic glory in Italy and England, lived there during the Hundred Days—the ancient Jacobin who had been intended for the priesthood, thinking perhaps how much happier he would have been if his mother's intention had been carried out. After the restoration the Palace was given back to the Orléans family and Louis, Philippe Égalité's son, was living there at the time of the 1830 Revolution, which carried him to the Tuileries as the Citizen King. Louis Philippe lives in history as a dull figure compared with the histrionic Bonapartes who preceded and followed him, but he was not without a touch of wit. When he was told of Talleyrand's death he asked if it was certain that he was really dead. "Quite certain, sire," was the reply; "did not your Majesty notice yesterday that he was dying?" "I did," said the King, "but there is no judging from appearances with Talleyrand, and I have been asking myself for the last four-and-twenty hours what interest he could possibly have in departing at this moment."

During the Second Empire the Palais-Royal was handed over to Jérôme Bonaparte, Louis Napoleon's uncle, whom his great brother had made King of Westphalia, and who was the most vicious and the most incompetent of the Bonaparte family. He and his son, Prince Napoleon, aptly described as the most prodigiously intelligent and prodigiously vicious man who ever lived, were sore trials to the man of Sedan, difficult even for his cynical forbearance to endure. Jérôme once sneered because his nephew had nothing of the great Napoleon about him. " Pardon me, my uncle," said the Emperor, " I have his family." Old man as he was, he scandalised even the Paris of Offenbach by living at the Palais-Royal with a red-headed enchantress who had him completely under her thumb. And his looks belied him. No one could think ill of the old gentleman always dressed in neat black with the Legion of Honour, the Iron Crown and—the inevitable touch of burlesque—his own crown of Westphalia, in his button-hole, coming to a fête in the Palais-Royal in honour of the Empress Eugénie, and leading her round the rooms, giving her, not his arm, but his hand, after the custom of his youth, and preceding her slightly with an antiquated but most chivalrous grace. Farce followed Jérôme almost to the grave. When he was dying a telegram was delivered to the Emperor at the Tuileries which read, " *Le vieux persiste*," which was a telegraphist's error for " *Le mieux persiste*."

There is history in the adjoining streets, particularly in the Rue de Valois, where Charles Lamb stayed during his visit to Paris, ordering an egg in bad French and being given a glass of brandy, which he received, it is said, with much pleasure, and where one can still dine excellently at the famous restaurant Bœuf à la Mode.

Near by is the first Duval restaurant that Paris ever knew, a spot of real historic interest, since Duval did for Paris what Sir Joseph Lyons did for London. And not far away is a draper's shop where the founder of the Bon Marché was once a shop-boy. It is odd to me that we do not pay greater attention to the lives of captains of commerce. It is curious that we know so little of Mr. Marshall or Mr. Snelgrove, and practically nothing of Mr. Swan and

THE PONT NEUF

Mr. Edgar. But there is one exception. Dufayel, who was a sort of Parisian Whiteley, built himself a most monstrous villa in the Champs-Élysées, which was used during the Paris Peace Conference as a Press Club. This gave Dufayel an international reputation, for he taught journalists from all over the world something, at least, of the extreme vulgarity of riches.

VI

THE BANKS OF THE SEINE

It is an interesting if somewhat protracted adventure to walk along the quays of the Seine from west to east on the right bank, returning from east to west along the left bank. The journey begins at the Quai d'Auteuil, a gloomy and depressing locality, and it has little interest until the Trocadéro is passed and the traveller has arrived at the Pont d'Iéna. Near the Trocadéro, by the way, is the Rue Franklin where, in quite a humble apartment on the *rez-de-chaussée*, M. Clemenceau lived during the latter days of the War and during the Peace Conference, when he was the virtual dictator of France.

The Pont d'Iéna was built in 1809. Its name, of course, is a reminder of Napoleon's overwhelming defeat of the Prussians. Old Blücher, whose manners Wellington found it so hard to endure after Waterloo, declared when he arrived in Paris that it was his intention to blow up the bridge, since its existence was an insult to his nation. But for once Louis XVIII. forgot he was a Bourbon and remembered that he was a Frenchman. He wrote to the King of Prussia begging him to forbid the vandalism of his Marshal and added that, if his request was refused, he would ask to be told the time at which the bridge was to be destroyed that he might place himself on the middle of it. One does not associate heroism with Louis XVIII., and it is possible that, if Blücher had had his way and the King had been advised of the hour of destruction, he would have reconsidered the matter and failed to keep his appointment. But he made a *beau geste* which saved the bridge.

The walk becomes delightful after passing the Pont de l'Alma, and Paris at its best with the tree-shaded quays,

PLACE DAUPHINE

the river with its Seine boats, like nothing else on earth, and the dignified elegance of the passers-by. The Pont Alexandre III., a modern bridge built to celebrate the alliance with Russia without which perhaps there would have been no Great War, is the newest of the Paris bridges and is evidence that the modern Frenchman is as great a bridge-builder as his forbears.

The Pont de la Concorde, over which the parliamentarian hurries to the sittings of the Chambre des Députés, was built in 1790 from the stones of the demolished Bastille. At the Pont des Arts the wanderer is in the very centre of historic Paris with the Louvre to his left, while across the river is the *quartier* of the poet and the artist. The Pont Neuf, despite its name, is the oldest bridge in Paris. It was begun in the reign of Henri III., the last of the Valois, and finished by Henri IV. Writing in his diary on Christmas Eve, 1643, John Evelyn says:

"Over the Seine is a stately bridge called Pont Neuf, begun by Henry III. in 1578, finished by Henry IV., his successor. It is all of hewn freestone found under the streets, but more plentifully at Montmartre, and consists of twelve arches, in the midst of which ends the point of an island, on which are built handsome artificers' houses. There is one large passage for coaches, and two for foot-passengers three or four feet higher, and of convenient breadth for eight or ten to go a-breast. On the middle of this stately bridge, on one side stands the famous statue of Henry the Great on horseback, exceeding the natural proportion by much; and, on the four faces of a stately pedestal (which is composed of various sorts of polished marbles and rich mouldings), inscriptions of his victories and most signal actions are engraven in brass. The statue and horse are of copper, the work of the great John di Bologna, and sent from Florence by Ferdinand the First, and Cosmo the Second, uncle and cousin to Marie de Médicis, the wife of King Henry, whose statue it represents. The place where it is erected is inclosed with a strong and beautiful grate of iron, about which there are always mountebanks showing their feats to idle passengers.

"From hence is a rare prospect towards the Louvre and suburbs of St. Germain, the Isle du Palais, and Notre-Dame. At the foot of this bridge is a water-house, on the front whereof, at a great height, is the story of our Saviour and the woman of Samaria pouring water out of a bucket. Above is a very rare dial of several motions, with a chime, etc. The water is conveyed by huge wheels, pumps, and other engines, from the river beneath. The confluence of the people and multitude of coaches passing every moment over the bridge, to a new spectator is an agreeable diversion."

The Place Dauphine, near the Pont Neuf, was named in honour of Louis XIII. by his father, Henri IV. Close to the Place was the famous Restaurant Magny where the famous literary dinners, of which Sainte-Beuve and the de Goncourts were the originators, were held in the middle of last century. Writing in their *Journal* of one of these dinners the de Goncourts record :

"An enormous discussion about God and religion, a discussion born of a good meal and good brains. Taine explained the advantages and the convenience of Protestantism to men of intellect, of the elasticity of its dogma, and of the interpretation which every one, according to his temperament, may give to his faith. He ended up by saying : 'At the bottom of it all, I believe these things are matters of sentiment, and I have an idea that musical natures are inclined towards Protestantism and plastic natures towards Catholicism.' "

The Tour St. Jacques, which the wanderer cannot miss, was built in the reign of François I., and was part of an old church pulled down in the Second Empire when the Rue de Rivoli was constructed.

The next bridge, the Pont au Change, derives its name from the fact that in the days when bridges were busy streets, it was the home of the goldsmith and the money-lender, and there is something suggestive in the fact that the bridge was burned down in 1621. Paris bridges, indeed, have had many casualties, the Pont Notre-Dame having bodily fallen into the river at the end of the fifteenth century. The Pont Neuf and the Pont au Change are frequently mentioned in the Dumas novels, and d'Artagnan and the three musketeers often swaggered across both of them. On the Quai du Louvre there still stands a café now called the Bouillon du Pont-Neuf, formerly known as the Café de Parnasse and the Café des Écoles, which was a rendezvous for students and young barristers who had

THE TOUR ST. JACQUES

only to cross the Pont Neuf to reach the Palais de Justice, and which Danton frequented in pre-revolution days when he was making his way at the Bar. The proprietor was one Carpentier, and in 1787, when he was twenty-eight, Danton married the patron's daughter Gabrielle, her father giving her a dowry of twenty thousand francs. Mr. Hilaire Belloc has written a vivid description of Danton at the time of his marriage :

" He was tall and stout, with the forward bearing of the orator, full of gesture and of animation. He carried a round French head upon a thick neck of energy. His face was generous, ugly, and determined. With wide eyes and calm brows, he yet had the quick glance which betrays the habit of appealing to an audience. His upper lip was injured, and so was his nose, and he had further been disfigured by the small-pox, with which disease that forerunner of his, Mirabeau, had also been disfigured."

The rest of the journey on the right bank is without any great interest. Coming back westward, near the Pont d'Austerlitz, the wayfarer passes the Jardin des Plantes, the poor Parisians' Zoo, where there is no charge for admission. It is not as interesting or complete as the London Zoo, but its peacocks have moved Mr. E. V. Lucas to admiration.

The Pont Sully joins the *rive gauche* to the smaller of the two Seine islands, the Île St. Louis. Here, on the Quai de Bourbon, Meissonier had his studio. The painter of military subjects was himself no mean soldier, but he was never quite happy because he was not elected a deputy or appointed a professor at the École des Beaux Arts. How quaint are men's ambitions !

Near by on the Quai de Bourbon both Baudelaire and Théophile Gautier lived for a time. Charles Pierre Baudelaire is as pathetic a figure as Villon or Verlaine. He was thirty-six when he published his famous *Fleurs du Mal*, and soon after he completed his translations of Edgar Allan Poe with whom he had so close affinity. He was always in pecuniary difficulties, and his debts compelled him to leave Paris for Belgium, where drink and opium led to his loss of reason. Like Guy de Maupassant, he died in a lunatic asylum. Baudelaire has been described as the first of the decadents, and he was the hero of the English decadent writers of the nineties of last century. He was, it has been well said, as afraid of life as was de Musset. But he was a very great poet, and it is good to remember his verse in this walk by the side of the Seine. There are memorable lines in Cyril Scott's translation of the *Fleurs du Mal*:

> A loudly echoing harbour, where my soul may hold
> To quaff, the silver cup of colours, scents and sounds,
> Wherein the vessels glide upon a sea of gold,
> And stretch their mighty arms, the glory to enfold
> Of virgin skies, where never-ending heat abounds.

Victor Hugo had a great admiration for Baudelaire's genius. He said in a letter to him: "*Vous dotez le ciel de l'art d'un rayon macabre, vous créez un frisson nouveau.*" Baudelaire, on the other hand, said of Hugo that the Almighty had taken in equal parts genius and silliness from which to compound the elder poet's brain so that in all his writing there was to be found an inexhaustible supply *de beauté et de bêtise*. There is a charming story told of Baudelaire visiting the Hugos when they were living in Brussels in 1864. Victor Hugo talked and Baudelaire was bored: "*Il gardait ses lèvres pincées, son regard aigu, sa dédaigneuse politesse, soigné de sa personne, net et muet.*" And then after a while he went to the piano and, despite Victor Hugo's notorious hatred of music, played "Tannhäuser" all through.

Swinburne's "Ave atque Vale," written in memory of Baudelaire, is one of the supreme elegies in our language. In one stanza there is a marvellous summary of the qualities of the French poet:

> Thou sawest, in thine old singing season, brother,
> Secrets and sorrows unbeheld of us:
> Fierce loves, and lovely leaf-buds poisonous,
> Bare to thy subtler eye, but for none other
> Blowing by night in some unbreathed-in clime;
> The hidden harvest of luxurious time,
> Sin without shape, and pleasure without speech;
> And where strange dreams in a tumultuous sleep
> Make the shut eyes of stricken spirits weep:
> And with each face thou sawest the shadow on each,
> Seeing as men sow men reap.

The de Goncourts wrote in 1857:

"Baudelaire has been supping next to us to-night.

L'INSTITUT

He wore neither tie nor collar, and his head was shaven, as if for the guillotine. In addition to this he has a studied elegance, little hands as carefully washed and trimmed as a woman's—and, to crown it all, a maniac's head, a voice that cuts like steel, and a delivery that aims at a sort of ornate exactness. He argues fiercely, with a sharp anger, that he has not put anything improper into his poems."

At the beginning of the eighteenth century, Le Sage, the author of *Gil Blas*, lived on the Quai de l'Horloge, hard by the Palais de Justice. Le Sage is an important person in the history of European literature. He stayed for a time at the French Embassy in Madrid and was well acquainted with Spanish romances which he used as the basis of his own writing. *Gil Blas* belongs to the same order of novel as *Don Quixote*, and with his picaresque and peripatetic novel—to use Major Hume's phrase—Le Sage had a strong influence on English writers. He, with Cervantes, was Fielding's master, and there is a direct connection between *Gil Blas* and *Tom Jones*. Le Sage was the most important French writer in the period between the great writers of the seventeenth century and the philosophers of the eighteenth. He was a retiring, independent man of letters, caring nothing for the patronage of the great. He was once invited to read one of his plays at the house of a duchess. He arrived late, and the duchess was rude, and Le Sage at once put his manuscript in his pocket and went home. The Théâtre Français refused his dramas, so he wrote scores of pieces for the Théâtre de la Foire, the booth playhouses that went from fair to fair. But though he wrote assiduously for the theatre, Le Sage can have had no great love for it, for when one of his sons went on the stage, his father disowned him. There was compensation, however, in the fact that another son was a Canon at Boulogne, and it was with him that the creator of *Gil Blas* passed the last days of his life.

Returning to the *rive gauche* and still going westward, one passes the Institut de France, built in 1663 as the Collège des Quatre Nations and endowed by Mazarin for the education of sixty poor scholars. The Bibliothèque Mazarine is still in the Institut, though most of the Cardinal's books are in the Bibliothèque Nationale in the Rue Richelieu, which stands on the site of the palace that Mazarin built when he had become powerful and wealthy. At an earlier part of his career Mazarin lived near the Institut on the Quai Malaquais. Three times in its history has France been governed by an Italian—by the Sicilian, Giulio Mazarini, and by the Corsican, Napoleon Bonaparte, and by the Genoese, Gambetta. There was none of the tremendous awesome dignity of Richelieu in the smooth Cardinal, but he must have been a man of infinite charm. "I have never approached the Cardinal," said Father Tixier, "without being persuaded I was going to talk to the greatest impostor in the world, and I never left his presence without being charmed by him." "He played his cards so well," said Cardinal de Retz, who hated him, "that he had his foot on everybody's head while everybody thought that he was still standing beside them." Mazarin died in 1661, leaving an enormous fortune. Towards the end of his life "the councils were held in his chamber while he was being shaved or dressed, and often he would play with his bird or his pet monkey while people were talking business to him."

In 1793 the College was used for the meetings of the Committee of Public Safety which, with Danton as its leader, saved the young Republic. Generals with royalist sympathies had turned traitor, nine nations were allied together for the destruction of the Revolution, there was civil war in the provinces and incompetence and indecision in Paris when this Committee of six determined men with a leader of magnificent courage and patriotic zeal came into being to organise the nation for its defence and to extirpate its enemies. There is something fine in the decree, "All France and whatsoever it contains of men or resources is to be under requisition."

Napoleon created the Institut de France in 1806, making it the home of the five academies—the Académie Française, the famous society of forty literary immortals; the Académie des Sciences; the Académie des Inscriptions et Belles Lettres; the Académie des Beaux Arts and the Académie des Sciences Morales et Politiques. Many of the immortals who have worn the famous green uniform since the Académie Française was founded by Richelieu in 1635, have been very mortal and are now hardly names, while many of the greatest French writers whose im-

OLD HOUSES, QUAI DES GRANDS AUGUSTINS

mortality is assured were never among the *immortels*. Le Sage, Rousseau, Beaumarchais, Diderot, Stendhal, Balzac, Gautier, Flaubert, Zola, Daudet, de Goncourt, de Maupassant, were all rejected, though some of them tried hard for election, and Victor Hugo was ten years a candidate before he was elected. The Académie has always been conservative in its sympathies, and when it elected M. Clemenceau, the old man's instinctive Radicalism revolted. He was, so the story runs, sitting in his room in the Ministère de la Guerre when M. Paul Cambon came to announce his election. "*J'ai l'honneur, M. le Président du Conseil, à vous annoncer que vous êtes élu à l'Académie Française.*" The old man looked up and growled, "*C'est ridicule.*" "*Mais M. le Président du Conseil,*" protested the diplomat, "*maintenant vous êtes parmi les immortels.*" To which the comment was, "*C'est grotesque.*"

Near the Quai de Conti, Athos, musketeer and *preux chevalier*, lived, at a "respectable inn" called Au Grand Roi Charlemagne. Fouché, Napoleon's Minister of Police, lived on the Quai Malaquais, originally known as the Quai de la Reine Marguerite, and then Quai Mal Acquis, because Marguerite of Valois stole a large part of the Petit Préaux-Clercs on which to build her mansion. Fouché is a typical figure of the Revolution. The precocious, sickly son of a sailor, he began life as a schoolmaster and met Robespierre while he was still a lawyer at Arras. He made his first entry on the revolutionary stage when he was elected to the National Convention in 1792, and he soon became conspicuous for his atheistic zeal. Fouché was a great phrase-maker. Over the gates of cemeteries he wrote, "Death is an eternal sleep," and on returning to Paris after an orgy of guillotining in Lyons, he declared: "The blood of criminals fertilises the soil of liberty." He was skilful enough to avoid sharing the fate of Robespierre, and when the Terror came to an end and during the Directory, after having made a fortune as a dishonest army contractor, he began his career as Police Minister which he continued under Napoleon as Consul and Emperor, and after the Restoration, under Louis XVIII. Fouché was a cunning fellow, a political Vicar of Bray, "a coarser Talleyrand." He was a master plotter, a most efficient bureaucrat, incapable of loyalty, and yet, like Talleyrand, he showed over and over again that he cared at least a little for his country, and he was bold enough to oppose Napoleon on many occasions. He died at Trieste, the Duke of Otranto and a very rich man.

It is said, by the way, and the story is curious, that it was the Duke of Wellington who persuaded Louis XVIII. to send Fouché back to his old post at the Préfecture de Police. The qualities of the old Jacobin could hardly have commended him to the Iron Duke.

Louise de Kéroualle, Duchess of Portsmouth, mistress of Charles II. and ancestress of the Duke of Richmond, died in a house on the Quai Voltaire. According to Saint-Simon, her family plotted to secure for her the favours of Louis XIV., but the plot failed and she came to England in 1670 with Charles's sister, Henriette, Duchess of Orléans, apparently with instructions to capture the susceptible English King. She was the French agent in the negotiations that bound England to Louis XIV. She was indeed a very astute lady whose rapacity was remarkable even among royal mistresses. Evelyn writes in his diary in November 1670: "I now also saw that famous beauty, but in my opinion of a childish simple and baby face Mademoiselle Kéroualle, lately Maid of Honour to Madame, and now to be so to the Queen." But there was nothing very childish or simple about Louise, and at a later date Evelyn expresses his horror of her extravagance:

"Following His Majesty this morning through the gallery I went with the few who attended him, into the Duchess of Portsmouth's *dressing-room* within her bed-chamber, where she was in her morning loose garment, her maids combing her, newly out of her bed, his Majesty and the gallants standing about her; but that which engaged my curiosity was the rich and splendid furniture of this woman's apartment, now twice or thrice pulled down and rebuilt to satisfy her prodigal and expensive pleasures, whilst her Majesty's does not exceed some gentlemen's ladies in furniture and accommodation. Here I saw the new fabric of French tapestry, for design, tenderness of work, and incomparable imitation of the best paintings, beyond anything I had ever beheld. Some pieces had Versailles, St. Germain, and other palaces of the French King, with huntings, figures, and landscapes, exotic fowls,

THE BOOKSTALLS, QUAI DES GRANDS AUGUSTINS

and all to the life rarely done. Then for Japan cabinets, screens, pendule clocks, great vases of wrought plate, tables, stands, chimney-furniture, sconces, branches, braseras, etc., all of massy silver and out of number, besides some of her Majesty's best paintings.

" Surfeiting of this I dined at Sir Stephen Fox's and went contented home to my poor, but quiet villa. What contentment can there be in the riches and splendour of this world, purchased with vice and dishonour ? "

It is with Voltaire himself that the Quai that bears his name is most closely associated, for he died there in 1778 at the age of eighty-six. He reached Paris after a long exile of twenty-eight years on February 5, and was received with the homage of the Court, society and the world of letters. Carlyle says of his welcome home :

" With face shrivelled to nothing ; with huge peruke *à la Louis Quatorze*, which leaves only two eyes visible, glittering like carbuncles, the old man is here. What an outburst ! Sneering Paris has suddenly grown reverent ; devotional with Hero-worship. Nobles have disguised themselves as tavern-waiters to obtain sight of him : the loveliest of France would lay their hair beneath his feet. 'His chariot is the nucleus of a Comet ; whose train fills the whole streets' : they crown him in the theatre, with immortal vivats ; finally 'stifle him under roses,'—for old Richelieu recommended opium in such state of the nerves, and the excessive Patriarch took too much."

In March he attended a performance of his play *Irène* and was crowned with laurel in his box, and he died on the 30th of May. The legends concerning his death are all entirely apocryphal. The facts are that he was too ill to listen to the priests who came to his sick-room and that he died without being shriven. Professor Saintsbury suggests that it is " singular and unfortunate that he who had more than once gone out of his way to conform ostentatiously and with his tongue in his cheek should have neglected or missed this last opportunity." In his old age Voltaire had an amazing appearance. He was so extremely thin that Arthur Young once described him as " Satan, death, and sin." His nose was very long and his eyes very brilliant, and he was as much addicted to coffee drinking as Dr. Johnson was to tea. Writing of Voltaire as a literary artist, Mr. A. B. Walkley has said: "He discovered the short sentence. Ease, simplicity, lucidity, were his cardinal virtues. Never was there a lighter touch, a slyer wit, a more mordant irony. With ostensible innocence he unexpectedly stings." Witty mockery is the note of Voltaire's writing and in this he was the master of Anatole France. Voltaire's body was hurriedly buried in a graveyard in Champagne, but the Revolution, recognising what it owed to the philosopher, brought it back in great state to the Panthéon in 1791.

Chateaubriand was living on the Quai Voltaire soon after the publication of his *Génie du Christianisme* which, by a happy accident, appeared immediately before Napoleon's re-establishment of the Church in France. Chateaubriand may be roughly regarded as the father of the romantic movement in French literature. He stood for the revolt against the cold detachment of eighteenth-century philosophy and the brutal realism of the Revolution and the Empire. His religion was romantic. It was the beauty of ceremonial, the poetry of symbolism, the wonder of great cathedrals, that appealed to him. When the young romantics, the chief of whom were Victor Hugo and Alfred de Vigny, began to publish their verse in the *Muse Française*, Chateaubriand was their patron saint. In gratitude, he declared that Hugo, a boy poet of twenty-two, was an *enfant sublime*.

After the Restoration, Chateaubriand held various diplomatic positions, and was at one time or the other both Minister for the Interior and Minister for Foreign Affairs. He was as romantic as a politician as he was as a poet. He was insistent that France should fight Spain in order to restore a most pernicious tyrant, and he was equally insistent that France should fight Turkey to liberate Greece. He was indeed eager that French armies should again be triumphant in the field in order, as Mme. Duclaux has said, "to hide out of sight the disgrace of 1814, the dismay of 1815, the degradation and inferiority that no mere riches can efface from a vanquished people." It is easy indeed to understand the revolt of a man of his temperament against the dull, vulgar, intriguing Paris described by Dumas in *Monte Cristo*.

Chateaubriand lived to be eighty, but his old age was

THE DEMOLITION OF THE MORGUE

a time of discontent, disillusion and envy. He was essentially an egoist with a sterile heart, and he seems to have had little real affection for any one except for the beautiful Mme. Récamier, who tended him in his last years. Unhappiness is often the lot of the literary genius. I think of Chateaubriand, disgruntled and disappointed, and then I think of Alfred de Vigny, whose poems Sir Edmund Gosse has described as unflawed amethysts and sapphires, forsaking the world when he was thirty-eight to live for another twenty-eight years in retirement, without ambition, the martyr of a pessimism that resulted from the discovery of the faithlessness of his mistress!

The joy of the Quais of the *rive gauche*, particularly on a sunny day, is the famous bookstalls where collectors search for bargains and rarely find them. In his memoirs, Alexandre Dumas *père* has the following description of a Seine-side bibliomaniac:

"Bibliomaniac, evolved from *book* and *mania*, is a variety of the species man—*species bipes et genus homo*. This animal has two feet and is without features, and usually wanders about the quais and boulevards, stopping in front of every stall and fingering all the books. He is generally dressed in a coat which is too long and trousers which are too short, his shoes are always down at heel, and on his head is an illshapen hat. One of the signs by which he may be recognised is shown by the fact that he never washes his hands."

The longest of the Quais on the south side is the Quai d'Orsay and its most famous building is the Ministère des Affaires Étrangères. There, during the Paris Conference, the Foreign Minister received the Press correspondents in his room hung with Gobelin tapestry, regularly to fence with questions put to him, generally in execrable French, and there in the Salle de l'Horloge were held the two public meetings of the Conference which the Press demanded and at which nothing happened except set speeches from President Wilson, Mr. Lloyd George and M. Clemenceau. I have a lively recollection of the angry protests from Mr. Hughes, the Australian Prime Minister, when Clemenceau declared that the sitting was over before he had had the opportunity of delivering an important pronouncement which he had carefully prepared.

Infinitely more interesting than the Ministère des Affaires Étrangères is the Hôtel des Invalides, where in its magnificent tomb lies the body of the great Emperor. "*Je désire*," he wrote in his will, "*que mes cendres reposent sur les bords de la Seine au milieu de ce peuple que j'ai tant aimé*." Napoleon at St. Helena is the most pathetic figure in history, and the petty persecution to which he was subjected is one of the most shameful incidents in the history of England. The great prisoner never lost his dignity in his misfortune. He found, indeed, a greatness entirely different to the restless egoism that had characterised the days of prosperity. In St. Helena, as Mr. Philip Guedalla has suggested, Bonaparte invented Bonapartism, and he was its first martyr. Las Cases records his rather high-flown statement :

"We remain the martyrs of an immortal cause : millions of men weep for us, the fatherland sighs, and Glory is in mourning. We struggle here against the oppression of the gods, and the longings of the nations are for us. . . . Adversity was wanting to my career. If I had died on the throne amidst the clouds of my omnipotence, I should have remained a problem for many men : to-day, thanks to misfortune, they can judge of me naked as I am."

France soon grew weary of the Bourbons. The romantic poets were *plus royalistes que le roi* in so far as they yearned for glory and splendour and resented middle-class drabness, and they had an immense influence on their age. Napoleon died in 1821, and his death stimulated the Bonapartist cult. Mr. Guedalla says that Louis-Philippe, fearing the new spirit and in the endeavour to bolster up his dynasty, became the most enthusiastic Bonapartist in France. The Arc de Triomphe was completed, the figure of Napoleon was once more set on its pillar in the Place Vendôme, and in 1840 a frigate commanded by the King's son went to St. Helena to fetch back the ashes of the Emperor. There is, however, another story. It is said that O'Connell told Palmerston that he intended to suggest the restoration of Napoleon's remains to France in the House of Commons. Palmerston pointed out that such action might seriously inconvenience the existing French Government. But O'Connell cared nothing for the convenience of Louis-Philippe. Whereupon Palmerston hinted to the French

PONT MARIE

Ambassador that the King had better ask the English Government for the remains and gain the credit for what might appear an act of magnanimity. Thackeray has written a description of Napoleon's return, of which he was an eye-witness, and I agree with Mr. E. V. Lucas in detesting its unsympathetic flippancy. The body was brought up the Seine to Courbevoie from whence it was carried by road to Paris, through the Arc de Triomphe, down the Champs-Élysées, across the Place de la Concorde to the Invalides. That was on December 15, 1840, a bitterly cold day with the temperature eight degrees below freezing-point, and yet there were, it is estimated, a million people in the streets keeping themselves as warm as they could with hand-warmers and foot-stoves and other devices, and chanting a song to the *Premier Capitaine du Monde*, one verse of which ran :

> Du Nil au bord de la Tamise
> Devant lui l'ennemi fuyait ;
> Avant de combattre il tremblait :
> Voyons sa redingote grise.

The coffin was received at the Invalides by the King, who stood with a little group of Napoleon's Marshals. A requiem was sung, and for days the body lay in state guarded by veterans of the Imperial Army. Duroc and Bertrand, two of the most faithful of the Emperor's servants lie now on either side of the entrance to the tomb, and near by are the bodies of Joseph and Jérôme, the elder a man of capacity, over-tried by conditions, the younger a man who, from youth to extreme old age, rightly earned the contempt of all his acquaintance, a contempt which his great brother most certainly shared.

Close by the Invalides is the École Militaire to which Napoleon came in 1784, receiving his commission as junior lieutenant in a regiment of artillery a year later when he was sixteen.

The Champ de Mars may well bring the Seine-side wander to an end. Beyond it and until the city boundaries are passed is little of interest or adventure. It was on the Champ de Mars in 1790 that the great *autel de la patrie* was set up, patriots shovelling and digging in preparation for the *fête de la Fédération*, a great crowd gathered from all parts of France to celebrate the beginning of the new regime of liberty. The King, not a little bewildered, was there; Lafayette, on a white horse, still a popular hero, but soon to pass from the scene, was one of the central figures. Talleyrand was there in cope and mitre, wearing a tricolour belt, to say his last mass, three hundred thousand people watching, while the pitiless rain pelted down upon them. Sainte-Beuve relates that the Bishop, as he still was, whispered mocking words to Lafayette as he mounted the altar steps.

A few months later crowds were again on the Champ de Mars at a national funeral service for the patriots killed at Nancy, forty thousand Parisians marching from St. Antoine, the presage of what was to happen in the next two years. A year passed, and again a great assembly came together to sign the petition, drawn up by Danton, which lay on the Fatherland's altar, praying for the deposition of the King, to be dispersed towards the evening with some loss of life, not, as Carlyle says, to be forgotten or forgiven. Mme. de Staël was present on the Champ de Mars at the second fête of the Federation when Louis was compelled to swear the national oath, wearing a quilted cuirass under his waistcoat lest some patriot should become too enthusiastic.

And the last of the revolutionary scenes on the Champ de Mars, and the finest! Verdun was lost, the Fatherland was in danger. All France was to be mobilised, and Paris hurried to the Champ de Mars to have itself enrolled "unarmed and undrilled, but desperate in the strength of frenzy." It was on that same day that Danton, in the greatest moment of his life, entered the Legislative, and referring to the enemies of the Republic, made his immortal challenge, "To conquer them to hold them back what do we require? *Il nous faut de l'audace, et encore de l'audace, et toujours de l'audace.*"

Since the Revolution the Champ de Mars has become the home of one international exhibition after the other, and has been disfigured by the Tour Eiffel. It is comforting that the invention of wireless telegraphy has provided some excuse for the existence of its monstrous ugliness.

So the Seine flows on through the city with perhaps more history stored on its banks than on the banks of any other river in the world.

VIEW FROM QUAI HENRI IV.

VII

NOTRE-DAME

WHEN I stand before the great west front of Westminster Abbey I think of Edward the Confessor, the monarch, saint and fool, to whom we owe the beginnings of the great Abbey Church of St. Peter, and who would, were he permitted once more to stand upon the banks of the Thames, be appalled by the rubbish with which his church is now encumbered. At Rheims I think of St. Joan of Arc, the sturdy peasant mystic, a realist incapable, as most mystics have been, of sentimentality and shilly-shallying, who took a coward prince, as it were, by the scruff of his neck and compelled him to become a crowned king. At Lincoln it is St. Hugh, with his St. Francis-like love of birds and beasts, that comes to my mind. Who can think of any one but St. Thomas at Canterbury, his fine courage giving romance to what, alas, has become a dull fane, and who at Chartres, most beautiful of all cathedrals, can think of any one but the master builders of the Middle Ages who, in an inspired co-operation, gave Europe the greatest of her treasures?

But Notre-Dame de Paris, standing on a bleak wind-swept square, is most intimately associated, not with a saint or a builder, but with a writer of romance, not with St. Louis, who brought to his city of Paris the Crown of Thorns, but with Victor Hugo. It is his cathedral, for so great is the power of the writer of fiction that he may steal from the rest of the world what he will, and if his genius be great enough, what he steals remains his until the end of time. Goswell Road belongs to Dickens—no one will grudge him its possession—because Mr. Pickwick lodged there with Mrs. Bardell. Wessex is no longer the kingdom of Saxon chieftains, but of Thomas Hardy. And in Notre-Dame we forget the kings and the emperors who have been crowned there, the brawling mobs who have desecrated the cathedral's sanctity and, until by strenuous effort we escape from the thraldom of romantic association, think only of Quasimodo in the bell tower, of the saturnine Frollo, and the hapless Esmeralda.

It was not by hazard that Victor Hugo appropriated Notre-Dame. For him, at the beginning of the romantic era in French literature, the cathedral was a consolation and an inspiration with its gloomy aisles and its suggestion of sinister mystery, with its grinning devils hovering near the sculptured figure of Our Lady. France had passed through the Revolution and the Empire. The logical theorists had had their day. There had been excitement, constitutions by the dozen, conquests and defeat. Such literature as the Revolution had produced was to Hugo hideous and inept, and in the creation of romance he turned for a model to the supreme creation of Gothic architecture, with its order in gigantic chaos. Victor Hugo knew every inch of the cathedral that he loved, and his description of it is the finest prose that he ever wrote.

But Notre-Dame is greater than Victor Hugo, and it has one quality which he sadly lacked. There is humour in the grinning devils on its façade—there is humour in all the great work of man—but there is no humour in Victor Hugo, in his writing or in the man. Think of him in his old age, the "Buddha on the bracket," as Mme. Duclaux has called him, gorging himself with the adulation of the foolish, bewildered by foreign worshippers like Swinburne, posing to the end, writing in his will, "I believe in God. I refuse the service of the churches. I beg a prayer from every soul." The grinning devils must have grinned a little more broadly when they read that will.

But, indeed, the adventurer must escape for a while from Hugo and from Hugo's by no means reliable history, if he is to find in Notre-Dame all the thrills that it enshrines. Victor Hugo asserts that the foundation of the cathedral was laid by Charlemagne, but as a matter of historical fact it was three hundred and fifty years after the death of the great Emperor that Pope Alexander III., who properly humbled the English King Henry II. for the murder of

NOTRE DAME

St. Thomas of Canterbury, exiled from Rome through the intrigues of Barbarossa, laid the first stone of the Cathedral of Paris. He was the guest of Louis VII., a King who himself had had uncomfortable experiences of the Papal power, having been laid under an interdict by Innocent II. The cathedral stands on the site of two ancient churches, built on the site of a temple dedicated to Jupiter. Notre-Dame was not completed until a hundred years after its commencement, when St. Louis, every inch a man and every inch a saint, sat on the throne of France. Before the building was completed, St. Dominic, of all missionaries most maligned by partisan history, had preached from its pulpit.

For seven hundred years Notre-Dame has been intimately connected with the story of France. It has been the stage on which each outstanding figure has strutted for his little hour, and it does not require any excessive imagination to stand in its aisles and to conjure up one vision after the other of what has happened under the vaulted roof. King Henry VI. of England, a boy of ten, was crowned King of France in Notre-Dame, but though Joan had been burnt at Rouen, the nationalism that she had aroused was ever growing stronger, and the boy King, soon, it is rumoured, to be with Joan numbered with the saints, was smuggled out of France with his attendant bishops and dukes to live a long, sad life in England and to dower it with schools and colleges. He must have been a frightened little figure on that December morning when he was acclaimed king of a people who would have none of him.

A century passes, and another winsome British-born personage, Mary Queen of Scots, walked up the aisle of Notre-Dame to be married to the Dauphin, afterwards Francis II., the eldest son of Catherine de Médicis. Mary was then sixteen, "*le plus parfayt enfant que je vys jamaes*," and as she stood at the altar, tall and fair, in heavy blue velvet robes and a golden coronet, she appeared to an observer "a hundred times more beautiful than a goddess in heaven." Who of the princes and the nobles in the cathedral, and the citizens who acclaimed the royal pair at the banquet in the Palais de Justice, realised that they were taking part in the prelude of a very tragic drama? Two years afterwards her wretched, sickly husband died, and the French chapter of Mary's life, with its laughter and gaiety, came to an end, and she went back to Scotland to meet John Knox—and her fate.

Henry of Navarre, great soldier, shrewd statesman, good European—did he not dream of a League of Nations in the sixteenth century?—and more even than most kings, enthusiastic amorist, came in state to Notre-Dame, publicly to proclaim his submission to the Catholic Church. To his sturdy Protestant mother, Jeanne d'Albret, that submission would have been unforgivable. But his mother was dead, and to Henry's practical mind, Paris that morning seemed well worth a mass.

Notre-Dame was hung with the flags that celebrated the victories of Louis XIV., victories to be paid for at the Revolution. And when the great Condé died in 1687, Bossuet, the greatest of French preachers, who was dreaming of the reunion of Christendom, as good men are dreaming of it now, preached one of his famous funeral orations from the pulpit of Notre-Dame, on the death of the soldier whose victory at Rocroy established French military supremacy on the continent of Europe.

Louis XIV., safely guarded by de Maintenon, died after an old age of austerity, repenting for both La Vallière and de Montespan. Louis XV.'s reign, dominated first by La Pompadour, a woman of some vision and character, and afterwards by Du Barry, little more than a slut, came to an end. The armies of France were defeated in India and Canada, and the story of the Bourbons drew to an end.

One more scene before the curtain rang down in confusion. Louis XVI., that amiable incapable, with his Queen Marie Antoinette (and no more pathetic figure since Mary Queen of Scots had entered the cathedral) and his child daughter, Elizabeth, went to Notre-Dame to offer thanks for the birth of the Dauphin, the poor little boy whose home was to be a prison and whose death a mystery. Then 1789, and the devils of Notre-Dame grinned and waited.

Four years after the fall of the Bastille the Revolution, that had already swept away so many things, invaded the Cathedral of St. Louis. Gobel was the Convention Bishop of Paris—called "goose Gobel" by Carlyle, apparently because he was born at Strasbourg. In the Convention the

THE PETIT PONT

"goose" tore off his episcopal raiment and declared that in France there should be no religion but liberty. Carlyle has told the story of what followed with incomparable skill, the bestial dawning of the age of reason, the destruction of sacred vessels, the turning of albs into shirts, the burning of relics, the insane orgy of atheism which, happily for France, was soon to pass. The culmination was the decree that Notre-Dame should become the temple of the new cult. The image of Our Lady was taken down, statues of Voltaire and Rousseau took the place of images of the saints, and a well-rouged ballet-dancer from the Opera was carried in state into the cathedral as the Goddess of Reason. Before the great doors of the cathedral a heap of breviaries and Bibles was set alight. But the Goddess had no worshippers. The new religion soon became a bore, and Notre-Dame was used as a storehouse for empty casks.

With Napoleon the cathedral was restored to its sacred purpose and, incidentally, played its part in advertising the glory of the Corsican. In 1804 Notre-Dame saw one of the most dazzling and also one of the most bizarre of the scenes of its long history. With pomp and circumstance Napoleon and Josephine were crowned Emperor and Empress of the French in the cathedral, the Pope himself being compelled to journey from Rome to grace the ceremony. It was with Pius VII. that Napoleon had concluded the Concordat that had brought the disorders of the Revolution to an end and restored to the Church at least a part of its possessions and its rights. But whatever gratitude the sovereign Pontiff may have felt must have been materially mitigated by the arrogance with which Napoleon made it clear that it was for him to command and for the Pope, with the rest of the world, to obey. Pontiff and Emperor met on the high road near Fontainebleau. The Pope, weary from his journey, was obliged to get out of his carriage and stand in the mud to be received by the Emperor. Afterwards he took the lower place in the Imperial carriage. Dumas has described the talks between them that preceded the coronation, Napoleon alternately cajoling and threatening, the Pope, immobile and bored, merely commenting *comediante* and *tragediante* as one mood passed into another. Notre-Dame was very cold on the morning of the coronation, and the Emperor kept the Pope waiting, chilly and apprehensive, and at the culminating moment of the ceremony when, after having anointed the Emperor and Empress with the holy oil and having blessed their crowns and rings, Pius was about to place the crown on the Emperor's head, he was waved aside, and Napoleon crowned himself.

There was nothing wanting in splendour in the scene. The Emperor himself glittered with jewels, the Empress looked resplendently beautiful in her robe of white satin. Around them were grouped the personages of the new Court—first-class fighting men come from the people, bearing resounding titles a little awkwardly—Grand Chamberlains, Grand Marshals, Grand Masters of the Hounds who, ten years before, were Jacobins and regicides, and some of whom had acclaimed the berouged goddess. There, too, was Napoleon's family—Madame Mère, that steely-nerved old woman, only one degree less wonderful than her son, the brothers puffed up and preening, Joseph's wife furious that she had to bear Josephine's train, and only consenting when she was bluntly told that the punishment for refusal would be exile in Germany. Fouché, the plotter, was in the throng, and Talleyrand, the master cynic, now dubbed Grand Chamberlain, and surely grinning behind his hand. And, as always at Notre-Dame, a figure of tragedy and pathos was in the centre of the picture. It was the culminating day in the career of Josephine de Beauharnais. Two days before she had been married according to religion, the first marriage being merely a civil contract, by Cardinal Fesch, her husband's uncle, and she may have persuaded herself that her position was secure. At Aix-la-Chapelle she had been offered the arm-bones of Charlemagne, and she had proudly replied that she would not deprive the city of them since she had the support of a greater than Charlemagne. But as Emperor and Empress ascended the throne, weighed down by their mantles, they stumbled and nearly fell, and Josephine, who had already heard whispers of divorce, must have regarded the stumble as an omen, and have left the cathedral with a heavy heart.

On April 2, 1810, Josephine having been divorced, Napoleon married, in Notre-Dame, Marie Louise of Austria. For Napoleon, after his coronation, there remained ten more years of glory, and then Waterloo and St. Helena, and Louis XVIII., the dullest and least mischievous of the

SAINTE CHAPELLE

later Bourbons, back in Paris, attending Mass in Notre-Dame and offering thanks for his restoration. But the Bourbons were unbearable, and the 1830 revolution brought Louis-Philippe, the Citizen King, to the French throne. The king's umbrella and the bourgeois trappings of his Court reinvigorated the Napoleonic legend. The eyes of France were turned to the lonely island in the south Atlantic. In 1840 another solemn service in the cathedral celebrated the coming home of the Emperor's remains for burial in the Invalides. The power of the legend increased and, stimulated by eager plotters, in 1848 Louis-Philippe was in not uncomfortable exile in England and the great Napoleon's nephew was Prince President. To me Napoleon III. is far more the man of destiny than Napoleon I. The uncle was a man of supreme genius and unbridled ambition, the architect of his own career, who sought power and loved it, who was at once, as are many men, a reckless egoist and a supreme sentimentalist. Louis Napoleon was from his youth convinced that fate intended him to reign in his uncle's place. He was a good-humoured, tolerant, disillusioned cynic, quite without morals of any kind, extraordinarily able, but if he had genius at all it was a genius for being bored. The *coup d'État* made him Emperor, but power, position, responsibility, all wearied him. Of all the outstanding figures of the nineteenth century he was supremely Mr. Facing-Both-Ways—a Liberal who made himself a tyrant, a man who never really knew his own mind and who always wished he had taken some other course than that which he had adopted. In 1853 he was forty-five. He had dull eyes, drooping moustache and pallid complexion. The Emperor must have an Empress, and Napoleon, after various snubs from German reigning families, selected the beautiful Eugénie de Montijo, a woman of supreme beauty and the smallest possible intelligence. It was a love match, so Napoleon told his Parliament, speaking French with a German accent, as his uncle had spoken with an Italian accent, and Palmerston, Napoleon's peer in cynicism, approved this choice of a beautiful woman since " he had no chance of a political alliance of any value or of sufficient importance to counterbalance the annoyance of an ugly or epileptic wife whom he had never seen till she was presented to him as a bride." France resented the alliance. She would have preferred some sort of a princess, ugly or epileptic though she might have been, for Empress. So the Herald's College was kept busy, and a Doge of Genoa, a Queen of Portugal and a King of the Asturias were discovered among Eugénie's collateral ancestors.

The marriage took place in Notre-Dame on January 30, 1853. The Emperor and Empress drove to the cathedral in the coach of glass and gold that had carried Napoleon and Josephine to their coronation. Behind them rode King Jérôme and Prince Napoleon in the coach which had borne the unfortunate little King of Rome to his baptism. Eugénie wore the diamond coronet that Marie Louise had worn on her wedding day, and Napoleon his uncle's insignia of the Legion of Honour. The scene was gorgeous, but the crowd was cold. There was no enthusiasm, "coarse jests passed from mouth to mouth," and in the evening the bride was hooted. And yet another omen. As the Imperial carriage was passing through the archway of the Tuileries, the gilded crown that surmounted it fell to the ground.

So as I pass out of the Cathedral of Notre-Dame de Paris into the great bare square, it seems to me that the cathedral is haunted by the ghosts of unhappy women who stood for a brief hour in glory and splendour within its walls as the prelude to heartbreak and disappointment. And, unlike most of the great ladies of history, these women of Notre-Dame have all been surpassing fair. Mary Queen of Scots walked down the steps of the cathedral to begin a journey that ended on the scaffold of Fotheringay Castle. Marie Antoinette went from the altar where she had offered thanks for the birth of her child to the Temple prison and the guillotine. Two years after she had been crowned the Empress Josephine was degraded, to eat out her heart at Malmaison. Marie Louise was married to become merely a troublesome political proposition. Seventeen years after her marriage to Napoleon Eugénie de Montijo endured Sedan and began an exile of long weary years, made greyer by the tragic death of her only son. And the men of Notre-Dame were no luckier. For the boy Henry VI. there was a long life of trouble and disappointment and a violent death. For Louis XVI., the guillotine. For the first Napoleon, Waterloo, and for his nephew, Sedan.

The most famous and the saddest of the stories of Notre-

THE CONCIERGERIE

Dame has nothing to do with kings or queens or emperors. It was in the house of one of the cathedral's canons that Peter Abélard, a man of thirty-eight and already a famous philosopher teaching in the cathedral school, met the canon's niece, Héloïse, a girl of seventeen, and at once forgot his philosophy. Abélard lived for twenty-six years after he fell in love with Héloïse, and they were years of shame, physical and mental suffering, insistent persecution, made beautiful at the end by the writing of the immortal letters which have caused Abélard and Héloïse to be remembered among the great lovers of the world. The tomb in which they lie together in the cemetery of Père Lachaise is a place of lovers' pilgrimages, for it was a miracle indeed that preserved their dust together through all the troubles of France. And who of the lovers remembers that Abélard remained a philosopher, that he was one of the teachers who first gave Paris its fame as a place of learning, and that the school that he opened at Mont St. Geneviève is said to have been the beginning of the Latin Quarter and its scholastic traditions?

Notre-Dame stands at one end of the Île de la Cité, the oldest part of Paris, and the Palais de Justice at the other, cathedral and Law Courts being separated by the Hôtel-Dieu, a building of beneficence, and the gloomy Préfecture where, during the War, foreigners spent hideous hours waiting for visas. But even the Préfecture has a suggestion of romance, for was it not the home of Lecoq, Vidocq and those other amazing detectives whose adventures have solaced many tiresome hours?

The Palais de Justice is magnificently situated, and if I had to go to law, which Heaven forbid, it would be more exciting to have the Paris Palais de Justice for the scene of the trial than the menacing Courts with their twisting passages that stand in the Strand. The Palais de Justice has for centuries played its part in the life of the French capital, and the beautiful Sainte Chapelle which used to contain the relics brought by St. Louis from the Holy Land dates back to the thirteenth century. The Salle des Pas Perdus is interesting to the foreigner because it is so noisy, so extremely un-English, lawyers and clients shouting at each other at the top of their voices, with none of the solemn hypocrisy associated with English legal proceedings.

But I have a common man's terror of law and lawyers, and no law court is a place that I should select in which to spend a happy day. It would fill a book to give a list of the *causes célèbres* that have been tried in the Palais de Justice. Passing it I recall the fact that France since the Revolution has largely been governed by lawyers. Danton and Robespierre were both lawyers, so were Thiers, Olivier, Gambetta, Poincaré and a host of others. When a French statesman is not a lawyer he is generally a journalist. Often he is both.

The Conciergerie prison which is part of the Palais de Justice has a host of tragic memories. Here in the courtyard Madame de la Motte, who plotted with Cardinal de Rohan about the diamond necklace, to Marie Antoinette's undoing, was publicly whipped and branded.

The terrible Tribunal Révolutionnaire, with Fouquier-Tinville as its prosecutor, had its sittings in a room in the Conciergerie, and there Marie Antoinette, Charlotte Corday and a host of others went for mock trial and certain condemnation. There is nothing in human records comparable with the proceedings before the Tribunal Révolutionnaire, except the almost similar proceedings that have taken place in recent years in Russia, and it is natural that Fouquier-Tinville, really a rather dull, conscientious lawyer, who was responsible for the Acts of Accusation, should be described in history books as " venomous as a serpent and sanguinary as a tiger," and should be denounced by the historians as a " cannibal." But none the less he was a good husband and father, and Louis Blanc has declared : " *Il sortit de la Révolution plus pauvre qu'il n'y était entré*." Fouquier was a lawyer—and it is only the rare lawyer who declines to administer the law, however horrid it may be.

PLACE ST. MICHEL

VIII

THE LUXEMBOURG AND ITS NEIGHBOURHOOD

THE Luxembourg is almost at the centre of what is to me the most interesting of all the Paris *quartiers*. Here, with the Boulevard St. Michel its main thoroughfare, is the Quartier Latin of Henri Mürger and romance. The famous Bal Bullier is not far away. Every street has its suggestion of the light-hearted student as well as of the achievements of the poet and the painter. But there is little of the Henri Mürger glamour in the Quartier Latin nowadays. Bohemia crossed the river long ago to the hill of Montmartre, though a province of it, rather mannered and unattractive, may be found higher up the hill on the south side of the river, at Montparnasse and Montrouge, where, however, a great many of the quaintly garbed youths are the revolting sons and daughters of the Puritan Republic of the West whose zeal for personal freedom is more obvious than their knowledge of the language of France.

The Musée du Luxembourg is the home of modern art, and the adjoining Palais du Luxembourg is the meeting-place of the Senators of the Third Republic, for the most part elderly and substantial gentlemen, whose habit it is to lunch admirably at the famous Restaurant Foyot that stands at the corner of the Rue de Tournon on the site of an ancient hotel where, in more picturesque times, kings and princes of France used to sup discreetly with more or less undesirable acquaintances.

The Luxembourg was built by Marie de Médicis during her brief period of power after the death of Henri IV., and one small part of the original building remains ; indeed this remnant may be part of an older hotel belonging to the Duc de Luxembourg from whom

Marie de Médicis bought the site. Marie bequeathed the palace to her second son, Gaston d'Orléans, and until the Revolution it was generally the residence of Monsieur, the King's eldest brother.

At the Revolution the Luxembourg became a prison, and it is sometimes related, with attractive inaccuracy, that when Josephine de Beauharnais took up her residence in the Palace after Napoleon had been proclaimed First Consul, she was returning to the prison that she had left five years before. But it was actually in the adjacent Carmelite monastery that de Beauharnais, with his wife and Hoche and a multitude of others, were imprisoned by the Terrorists. De Beauharnais was a handsome aristocrat and a prominent figure in the early days of the Revolution. It was he who was chosen to interrogate Louis XVI. after the futile flight to Varennes. Afterwards he fought with some distinction in the revolutionary armies, not forgetting to record his own prowess in his dispatches. He took his part in 1790 in the strange scene on the Champ de Mars, when soldiers and politicians and patriots all worked with pick and shovel to build the *autel de la Patrie*. But for all his shovelling and fighting de Beauharnais remained an aristocrat, and to prison he went and thence, after three months, to the guillotine. He seems to have borne himself with dignity and courage, but Josephine was no stoic. Her months in prison were months of trembling and tears, with hours spent in the endeavour to discover her fortune from the cards, and now and again, so scandal says, with episodes of love-making. Josephine had friends among the Terrorists and her charm and beauty were sufficient to conquer even their hearts. A fortnight after her husband's execution she was at liberty again to face an interval of grinding poverty before, thanks to Madame Tallien, she attracted the fancy of Barras.

It was at the Luxembourg that Napoleon was received by the Directoire Government when he returned to Paris after the campaign in Italy. A temporary " altar of the country," surrounded by the statues of Liberty, Equality and Peace, was set up with a huge grand stand for the accommodation of the patriotic sightseers. Napoleon was embraced by Barras and eulogised by Talleyrand, and he replied in a flowery speech in which he declared : " You

THE LUXEMBOURG GARDENS

have effected the organisation of the great nation the territory of which is only circumscribed because nature itself has fixed its limits." But Napoleon was not yet the idol of the people and Paris was more curious than enthusiastic. Moreover, the occasion was marred by the falling of one of the Directoire clerks from the top of the stand during the patriotic orations.

After the reception Napoleon went to live quietly, awaiting his time, in a house in the recently renamed Rue de la Victoire, a street parallel with the Rue La Fayette, at the top of which most travellers from England make their entrance into Paris, and which is incidentally one of the longest, and one of the dullest, streets in Europe. With the three million francs collected during the Italian campaign, Napoleon was no longer the poverty-stricken unemployed soldier who, two years before, had waited in Barras's anteroom, but in the Rue de la Victoire, thanks to the spying and whispering of his family, he had the first furious and not unreasonable jealous quarrels with his wife.

It was to the Luxembourg again that Napoleon went as First Consul, occupying a suite of rooms on the ground floor to the right of the entrance from the Rue de Vaugirard. This was the beginning of one of the most interesting episodes in the most bewildering of all careers. Napoleon knew nothing about the business of government. He knew very little of the quality of the men from whom he had to select his ministers and administrators. If Bourrienne, his scheming secretary, is to be believed—and he rarely is—Napoleon was at this time genuinely anxious for peace, and particularly for peace with England, but the Courts of Europe would have no dealings with the upstart from Corsica, and it was not until after the victory at Marengo that the Peace of Amiens became a possibility. If the British Government had been wiser in 1799 it might have saved Europe from sixteen years of war, and the history of Europe would certainly have been vastly different.

During the first months at the Luxembourg, Napoleon learned to appreciate the great qualities of Talleyrand, the cynic who was always a patriot, the politician who was always changing his coat, and at the same time always contriving to serve his country. No man knew Napoleon better than Talleyrand. No man had a truer appreciation of his qualities and his deficiencies, and whatever else may be said of him, he remained faithful to his master until it was quite certain that he could no longer be faithful to him if he remained faithful to France.

In the Luxembourg Murat was privately married to Caroline Bonaparte. The marriage took place at a time when Napoleon was almost penniless, and he gave his sister as a wedding present a pearl necklace belonging to his wife. In view of the relations existing between Josephine and her sister-in-law, this did not add to his domestic bliss.

The Court of the Consulate, for four months at the Luxembourg and afterwards at the Tuileries, was a very different thing to the Court of the Directoire. Napoleon insisted on order and decency and dignity, and Josephine with her lovely voice and exquisite grace, which made men forget that her teeth were bad and that she was not strictly beautiful, accepted the new conditions and played her new part with complete success.

After the establishment of the Empire the Luxembourg began its period of respectable dullness. It housed the Imperial Senate, afterwards renamed the Chamber of Peers, to become during the Second Empire the Imperial Senate again, and now the Senate of the Republic. As I think of these years I recall the great scene which Dumas has imagined, when the beautiful Greek Haydée denounced the rascality of Fernand Mondégo, who was unanimously condemned by his colleagues.

The Musée du Luxembourg might well be called the Palais de Rodin. It contains his *Pensée*, his *John the Baptist*, and the heads of Hugo and Rochefort, George Wyndham and Bernard Shaw, with the great *Age of Bronze*. It has been finely said of Rodin's work : "These are no graveyard figures, but living men, moving and breathing in the air that surrounds them." "Everything," he himself once said, "is contained in nature, and when the artist follows nature, he gets everything."

Rodin had the habit of living and working in historic houses. For some time he had a studio on the Boulevard Auguste Blanqui, on the hills at the south of the city, in an eighteenth-century house that had once been used by Napoleon as a hunting-lodge, and was afterwards a hospital

LA SORBONNE

laundry. From there he went to the Boulevard des Invalides, to a house which had been the Paris home of the Ducs de Biron, who in their time played many parts in the history of France. One Duc commanded the Royalist forces at the siege of Rochelle. Another was concerned with the intrigues of the League and the wars of religion, finally to be convicted of high treason and beheaded in the Bastille during the reign of Henri IV. A third fought with Lafayette in the American War of Independence and afterwards did notable service with the French armies in Europe. He received the usual reward of the aristocrat soldier and was guillotined in 1793.

I return to the Luxembourg if only to pay tribute to the joy of the gardens, which remain much as they were laid out when the palace was built, and which, on Sunday afternoons, show *bourgeois* Paris at its very best—corpulent fathers of families vigorously playing games with their offspring and manufacturing their own rules.

Nowhere do the streets of Paris give the opportunity for meeting so noble a company of ghosts as here between the Seine and the Boulevard du Montparnasse, with the Boulevard St. Michel on the east and the Rue des Saints Pères and the Rue de Sèvres on the west. In the Rue de Tournon Balzac set up the printing press which ruined him. Near by, in the Rue Visconti, lived Gambetta, Daudet and, long before, St. Francis de Sales, held in high veneration by me, since he is the patron saint of my craft. It was in 1618 that St. Francis paid his third visit to Paris where he had spent many years of his youth and where he was already regarded as a saint. His constant companion was St. Vincent de Paul, that priest of many good deeds, chosen by Louis XIII. as Royal Almoner of the Galleys, who was a Royal Almoner indeed. And among his penitents was the famous Mère Angélique Arnaud. Few saints have ever been more honoured in their lifetime than St. Francis de Sales, who has been officially described in a Vatican pronouncement—and this is perhaps why he was selected as the patron-saint of journalists—as being "all things to all men." It is pleasant to remember that the *quartier*, not famous for its saintliness, once harboured so notable a saint.

Balzac lived in the Rue de Tournon from 1827 to 1830.

His whole life was one furious struggle to pay his debts, and his printing business landed him with liabilities which were a drag on him until he died. There is a particularly delightful story of Balzac in the de Goncourt *Journal*. The Marquis of Hertford, who spent most of his life in Paris and whose son, Sir Richard Wallace, bequeathed the Wallace collection to London, was extremely anxious to meet Balzac. He was told that the novelist was difficult and shy. But Hertford was a millionaire and not easily discouraged, and eventually an interview was arranged. Balzac, however, did not keep the appointment, and it was explained to Hertford that he was threatened with imprisonment for debt, and that he dare only go out in the evenings, since arrest was illegal after dark. " How much does he owe ? " asked Hertford. " A large sum," was the reply, " perhaps forty thousand francs, perhaps fifty thousand francs, perhaps more." " Well, tell him to come here and I will pay his debts."

Balzac worked prodigiously hard and lived frugally, but still he never had any money, and one of his intimates has explained why. " He embarked on the most harum-scarum speculations without the slightest particular knowledge ; as for instance when he drew the plans for his country house and insisted on the builder carrying them out in every respect while he was away. When the place was finished there was not a single staircase. Of course they had to put them outside, and he maintained that it was part of the original plan."

George Sand, who at one time lived in the Rue d'Assas and towards the end of her life in the Rue Racine, admired Balzac, but found him too outspoken for her taste. " You are a lewd fellow," she said to him once. " You are a beast," was the rejoinder, to which she replied, " I am well aware of it." The de Goncourts have a striking picture of George Sand as an old woman when they visited her in the Rue Racine in 1862 :

" Mme. Sand looks like an automaton. She talks in a monotonous and mechanical voice, which neither rises nor falls and never gets animated. Her attitude has something of the gravity, the placidity, the somnolence of a ruminant. Her movements are slow, very slow, almost like a somnambulist's, and they always lead to the same thing—always

RUE DE SEINE

with the same methodical actions—to the lighting of a wax match and to a cigarette at her mouth.

"Mme. Sand has been very kind to us, and has praised us a good deal, but with a childishness of ideas, a flatness of expression, and a sombre good-nature which have made us feel as chilly as if we were in an unfurnished room."

To return to the Rue de Tournon. It was in 1917 that Mr. Charles Whibley introduced me to what was its then most notable inhabitant, M. Tussieu, the barber whose proud boast it was that he had cut the hair of Hugo, Daudet and half the great French writers and painters of the last fifty years. Outside the shop was the inscription :

> Ici Monsieur Tussieu barbier
> Rase le Sénat,
> Accommode la Sorbonne,
> Frise l'Académie.

During the War M. Tussieu added :

> Bulgares de malheur
> Turques, Austro-Hongrois, Boches,
> Ne comptez sur Tussieu
> Pour tondre vos caboches.

I particularly remember the morning when I met M. Tussieu, for afterwards Mr. Whibley and I went to the Taverne du Panthéon for an *apéritif*, and there we gossiped with an elderly French *bourgeois* who—as all Frenchmen did during the War and as most Frenchmen do now—hotly denounced the politicians of his country, adding how much luckier we were to possess politicians who were both capable and honest. When the caustic author of Blackwood's *Musings without Method* assured him that the English politicians were even worse than the French variety, it was with the greatest difficulty that we prevented our French acquaintance from embracing us both.

Close to the Luxembourg is the Théâtre de l'Odéon, one of the State theatres, which was first built in 1782, twice to be burned and rebuilt, and which is still surrounded by fascinating bookstalls. Opposite the theatre is the Café Voltaire, which has been for two hundred years the meeting-place of men of letters, and where I once saw Verlaine.

Bookshops fill the arcades round the theatre and eager readers read as much as they can from the uncut pages of the new books. Anatole France says of these enthusiasts :

" These open-air readers must have plenty of imagination. They will shortly be going along the cold, black streets, finishing the interrupted sentence in a dream. And very likely they will make it more beautiful than the reality. They will carry away with them an illusion, a desire, or at least a curiosity. It is seldom that a book yields us as much when we read it through at leisure."

It was from No. 2 Place Voltaire that Camille Desmoulins was hurried off in April 1794 to the Luxembourg and then to the guillotine, his beautiful young wife hovering round the prison day and night, as Carlyle says " like a disembodied spirit."

Near the Odéon in the Rue des Cordeliers, Charlotte Corday stabbed Jean Paul Marat on July 17, 1793. Carlyle makes Marat the arch-villain of the Revolution. To Charlotte Corday, the Girondiste, he was a savage wild beast ; to Carlyle he is squalid, atrocious, and nothing more. The truth is that Marat was a man of great capacity, a physician with a St. Andrews degree, a student of politics who alone of the revolutionaries realised that eighteenth-century England was an aristocratic oligarchy and not a democracy ; an enthusiast who abandoned a good professional income to give his whole time and energy to the cause of the people, and who left exactly twenty-five francs when he died. Marat being a Frenchman was a realist, and he understood that it is impossible to have a revolution without sooner or later indulging in more or less wholesale executions. Revolutions are inconceivable without executions, and as the English temperament is unsympathetic to the guillotine and the gallows, I am convinced that a revolution in this country must be of necessity an ineffective waste of time and money. But although Marat demanded the execution of the enemies of the Republic, it is unlikely that he would have supported the September massacres of 1794 which were reasonless and actually destructive of the Revolution, and it is probable that, if he had lived, Danton, Camille Desmoulins, and perhaps even Robespierre would have been saved from the knife. That Marat had acute judgment is shown by his estimate of Robespierre : " He has the knowledge of a wise Senator and the integrity of a really good man as well as the zeal of an honest patriot, but his defects as a statesman are a dimness of vision and a

S. NICHOLAS DU CHARDONNET

lack of determination." Compare this with Mr. Belloc's picture: "He (Robespierre) stood a pale exception, a man all conviction and emptiness, too passionless to change, too iterant to be an artist, too sincere and tenacious to enliven folly with dramatic art or to save it by flashes of its relation to wisdom."

In this same neighbourhood, in the Rue de l'Abbaye there was another revolutionary prison in which Mme. Roland and Charlotte Corday both spent their last days. Charlotte Corday appeared, played her part, killing one man "to save a hundred thousand," and disappeared with almost inhuman calmness, unperturbed, courteously declining the ministrations of a priest, blushing when the executioner insisted that she should take the neckerchief from her neck, "most definite, most complete; angelic-demonic; like a star."

Close by again in the Rue du Four, Robespierre once lived, and Ernest Renan lived in the Rue de Mézières. I like to think of Renan, with Paris broken-hearted after the tragedy of Sedan, with the Emperor whom he hated a prisoner in Germany, calmly dining *chez* Brébant and eulogising his country's enemies. "In everything I have studied," he said, "I have always been struck by the superiority of German intelligence and work. It is not astonishing that in the art of war, which after all is an inferior art, but complicated, they have reached this superiority which I see in everything, I repeat I have studied, which I know. Yes, gentlemen, the Germans are a superior race." It is not surprising that philosophers are apt to be unpopular in war time.

Alfred de Musset lived in the Rue Cassette, the poet who had the appearance of a "dandy cavalry officer in mufti." The finicky grace of his poetry was characteristic of the man who always refused to take any coppers given him in change, a habit that was a sore trial to his economically minded brother Paul, who none the less had for him deep admiration and affection. When it was suggested to Paul, who was himself a writer of some distinction, that he should stand as a candidate for the Académie Française, he replied: "*C'est bien assez d'un immortel dans la famille.*"

In a tennis court in the Rue Mazarine, Molière opened his ill-fated l'Illustre Théâtre in 1643. The audiences were poor, and by the end of 1644 his company had deserted the dramatist actor-manager, and he was arrested on the plaint of a candlemaker, to whom he owed one hundred and forty-two livres.

Laurence Sterne boarded for a time with a French family in the Rue Jacob during his long stay in France from 1762 to 1764. He fell in love with Paris at first sight. As he was driving to the hotel in the Faubourg St. Germain, where he stayed on his first night, he translated the legend on the Louvre :

> Earth no such folks—no folks e'er such a town
> As Paris is—sing derry derry down.

In Paris Sterne met Diderot and the encyclopædists, was received by the Duc d'Orléans and preached at the British Embassy chapel. One always recalls Yorick's preaching with a little shudder, but his sermon in Paris seems to have been particularly good. In a letter to his daughter he said : " I have preached at the Ambassador's chapel—on Hezekiah (an odd subject your mother will say). There was a concourse of all nations and all religions too."

The most interesting of the churches in the neighbourhood of the Luxembourg is St. Sulpice, where Camille Desmoulins was married, with Robespierre as best man—a tragic wedding indeed—Camille young, enthusiastic, good-looking, his wife rich and beautiful, with Robespierre, the skeleton at the feast. St. Sulpice was built in the eighteenth century and is generally regarded as an example of the degraded taste of the time, but to Gibbon, who was typically eighteenth century, it was " one of the noblest structures in Paris." Victor Hugo had the same contempt for St. Sulpice as Dickens had for St. John's, Westminster. He said that its two towers reminded him of two enormous clarionets. The famous seminary of St. Sulpice was shut up by the State twenty years ago. The English may remember with some pride that among the more recent *séminaristes* was Cardinal Bourne, the present Archbishop of Westminster.

In the middle sixties of the last century in a wine-shop on the corner of the Rue Bonaparte and the Place St. Sulpice, a dining club called " Les Vilains Bonhommes," used regularly to meet once a week. Its members were the poets

ST. GERMAIN DES PRES

who were known as *Parnassiens*, among them Verlaine, Anatole France, François Coppée, who was to become famous as a defender of the Church; Catulle Mendès, whom many years afterwards I saw night after night writing theatrical criticisms for the *Matin* in the Café Napolitain; Villiers de l'Isle-Adam, always poor, always homeless, of whom Anatole France has said with his genius for painting his contemporaries: "He was of a livid colour splotched with red with a lack-lustre eye and the bowed back of the poor man"; and Stephen Mallarmé, the author of *l'Après-midi d'un Faune*, "a little brown gentle person," to quote Sir Edmund Gosse, who besides being a poet, was a teacher of English.

One evening Verlaine took with him to "Les Vilains Bonhommes" that most offensive young genius, Rimbaud, who was responsible for the most doleful incidents of his life. Rimbaud was dirty, uncouth, and intentionally ill-mannered. He received anything but a cordial welcome, and when he proceeded to interrupt when one of the poets was reading a "masterpiece," he was promptly told that he would have his ears pulled if he did not behave. Whereupon Rimbaud, who was half mad and almost a savage, seized a sword-stick, rushed at the poet and severely wounded him, and from that night neither he nor his introducer was admitted to the club.

The Parnassiens, whose movement was a revolt against romanticism, were roughly criticised by Barbey d'Aurévilly, already an old man, although he did not die till 1889, and who, beginning life as a worshipper of Byron, lived to be the last of the romantics. D'Aurévilly lodged for thirty years in the Rue Rousselet, just across the western border of this Luxembourg district. He must have been a strange and wonderful figure. When Anatole France was a small boy he met him at his grandmother's, "wearing over his ear a hat with crimson velvet edges, with his figure encased in an overcoat with puffed skirts, tapping the gold stripe on his tight trousers with a whip as he walked." Even in his old age he was seen in the streets of the *quartier* "in black satin trousers which fitted his old legs like a glove, in a flapping brigand wideawake, in a velvet waistcoat which revealed diamond studs, and lace cravat, and in a wonderful shirt that covered the most artful pair of stays."

Victor Hugo called d'Aurévilly an imbecile, but Anatole France regarded him with at least tempered admiration. His eccentricities, he said, were never malicious. He had a natural gift for eccentricity, and while Sir Edmund Gosse would have us believe that his room in the Rue Rousselet was sordid in its misery, Anatole refers to " the noble poverty " of that apartment.

D'Aurévilly's most interesting book is *Du Dandyisme de Georges Brummel.* He was the last of the dandies. Even Mr. Max Beerbohm has not had the courage really to revive the tradition. He belonged to the French writers of the nineteenth century who are sometimes called neo-Catholics and were the followers of Chateaubriand. While immensely impressed by ritual and paying lip homage to the Church, they paid little heed to its ethical injunctions. But Anatole France suggests that they will be gently treated in another world. He imagined that when the dandy met St. Peter, the saint said :

" Here is M. Barbey d'Aurévilly. He longed to possess all the vices, but failed ; for that is very difficult, and requires a peculiar temperament. He would have liked to wallow in crime, for crime is picturesque ; but he remained the kindliest person in the world, and his life was almost monastic. He has often said bad things, it is true ; but as he never believed them or made any one else do so, they remained nothing but literature, and his error may be pardoned."

Not far from St. Sulpice is St. Germain des Prés. The Abbey of St. Germain was founded in the sixth century by King Childebert in honour of St. Vincent, whose miracle-working coat he had taken from the people of Saragossa. There is a contemporary description of this great church with its roof sheathed in copper-gilt, which was dedicated to St. Germanus, Bishop of Paris, to whom it had owed as much as it owed to the king, and who was buried within its walls. Round it a whole district grew up, the district of what is now the Faubourg St. Germain, nowadays the home of such of the old French nobility as is left, with a great many more of the new profiteers.

Five centuries after its foundation the church, which had been partly destroyed three times by the Normans, was rebuilt, and there is nothing left now of the church of

ST. SEVERIN

Childebert and Germanus where Charlemagne, as a little boy of eight, walked in procession with a candle in his hand.

Returning eastward and crossing the Boulevard St. Michel, the wanderer discovers the Panthéon, which was built by Louis XV. as a church in honour of St. Geneviève. In 1791 it became the Panthéon and was dedicated *Aux grands hommes de France la Patrie Reconnaissante*. On April 4 of that year the body of Mirabeau was brought here, the funeral procession being a league long and the streets crowded with a hundred thousand mourners. But Mirabeau was not to stay in the Panthéon very long, for two years later his body was bundled out to make way for the ashes of Marat, carried there in a funeral car specially designed by the Jacobin artist David. Marat, who had hated Mirabeau and had denounced him as an aristocrat, stayed in the Panthéon an even shorter time. Less than a year and his dust was taken away to be hastily buried at Montmartre. " Shorter godhead had no divine man," comments Carlyle.

While Mirabeau lay in the Panthéon, a gloomy depressing building, he was joined by Voltaire, whose funeral procession would surely have given that cynic not a little amusement. On the funeral car was an effigy of the dead philosopher being crowned with laurels by a young girl, and fifty other girls dressed in the costume of the characters of his plays walked in the procession. But, unfortunately, on the day of the funeral there was a tremendous rain storm. The colour was washed off the face of the effigy, and the mourners were compelled to take shelter in convenient doorways.

Victor Hugo was buried in the Panthéon in 1885, after his body had lain in state under the Arc de Triomphe. His funeral was even more magnificent than Voltaire's. The hearse was humble and unassuming, but after it came delegation after delegation, representatives of the army, Parliament, the Academy with, as Madame Duclaux relates, " the Friendly Society of Ménilmontant, the Freemasons of Montmartre, the Gymnasts of Belleville (in their tights), Ba-Ta-Clan ' les Beni-bouffe-toujours.' " One of the crowd exclaimed as he watched the procession pass : " *Il serait content, le père*," and Madame Duclaux agrees that the procession would have delighted Hugo's Cyclopean humour, his vague humanitarianism, his Socialistic fervour, his eye for effect, his talent for staging enormous scenes.

Years afterwards Hugo, the romanticist, was joined by Zola, the realist, who was carried to the Panthéon, not as a literary man, but as the champion of Dreyfus, the honour causing considerable trouble and forcible protest from angry Nationalists.

Near the Panthéon there are two interesting churches. St. Séverin dates back to the sixth century. Severinus was a hermit who sheltered Clodwig, son of Clodomir, who lives in history as St. Cloud. Severinus was buried near the cell where he had lived and Clodwig built a chapel in his memory. The church was rebuilt in the time of St. Louis and is to-day famous for its wonderful glass—the subject of one of the windows is the Martyrdom of St. Thomas of Canterbury—and for the appeal written on the tower : *Bonnes gens qui par cy passez, priez Dieu pour les trépassés*. The dedication of the church has a curious history. In the fifteenth century the hermit was forgotten and the patron-saint became another Séverin, who was also the patron-saint of travellers. In his honour horseshoes were nailed on the church door. But in 1753 the hermit was again remembered, and the church is now under the patronage of both the Séverins.

St. Étienne du Mont is the church of St. Geneviève, the patron-saint of Paris. In this church, the history of which goes back to the sixth century, were kept the relics of the city's patron until they were burnt during the Revolution, and here, during the War, many prayers were offered to her that she should, as in former days, save the city from its enemies from across the Rhine.

S. ETIENNE DU MONT

IX

STARTING FROM THE BOULEVARDS

To the tourist the Grands Boulevards are the most interesting part of Paris, but only to the tourist, though even the sophisticated must realise the attractive dignity of the long stretch of street from the Madeleine to the Place de la République. The tourist, be it said, will probably turn round and walk westward again when he reaches the Rue Drouot, and if he is more enterprising, will rarely go beyond the Rue du Faubourg Poissonnière. I know no pleasanter way of spending an hour on a summer's day than in sitting outside the Café de la Paix, opposite the Opera and at the very centre of Paris, and just watching the people—people from all sorts of countries and in all sorts of clothes, the foreigners, varying from school-marms from the Middle West to strange Armenians, carrying over their arms the carpets that they never seem to sell—who on earth ever bought a carpet outside a café ?—and far outnumbering the native-born Parisians.

To the Parisian the least interesting part of his city must surely be the streets running immediately south from the Opera. The Opera House itself is said to be the largest theatre in the world. It was opened in 1875, taking the place of the theatre in the Rue Le Peletier that was burned down in 1873. On January 14, 1858, Orsini, " a bearded man from the Romagna," waited patiently outside this earlier Opera House for the arrival of Napoleon III. and the Empress Eugénie, who were to attend a performance of " William Tell." As the imperial carriage drew up three bombs were thrown, and the lights went out, and the streets were filled with broken glass. Neither the Emperor nor the Empress was hurt. They were received with vociferous enthusiasm as they entered their box, and again as they drove back to the Tuileries. The incident has both human and political interest. Orsini was a fervent Italian Nationalist. "His reasoning was confused," says Mr. Guedalla, "but it followed closely the teaching of Mazzini and the normal course of political conversation in back rooms in Soho." He had convinced himself in some queer way that Italy would never be free until Napoleon was killed. Hence the bombs outside the Opera House. Politically the incident was important, because it caused vehement protest in France against the harbouring of political conspirators in England according to the right of asylum so dear to the hearts of nineteenth-century Liberals, and the protest was the beginning of a coolness between the two countries, which grew more and more dangerous until the end of the reign of Queen Victoria. Napoleon, by the way, strangest of men who ever wore a crown, with his entire incapacity for resentment, actually supplied the *avocat* who defended Orsini with a letter received by him from the would-be assassin, which was read in court, and made the foolish fellow appear something of a patriot.

In front of the idler sipping an *apéritif* outside the Café de la Paix, is the Rue de la Paix with its shop windows full of costly goods which no one really need buy, and the street is only really humanly interesting at the hours when it is filled with the chattering little *midinettes* who are the true Parisiennes and far more attractive than the millionairesses from North and South America who buy the goods that they make.

The Place Vendôme, at the bottom of the Rue de la Paix, was originally laid out as a monument to the glory of the armies of the *Grand Monarque*. It was first called Place des Conquêtes, to be renamed Place Louis le Grand, when a statue of the King was set up in it. Napoleon erected the column in the centre of the square, made out of cannon taken from all the armies of Europe. After the Restoration the statue of the Emperor was pulled down from the top of the column and remoulded into the statue of Henri IV., which is now on the Pont Neuf. Another statue of the Corsican, however, was erected by Louis-Philippe, and a better one by Louis-Napoleon. The column was pulled down by the Communards and set up

L'OPERA

again in the early days of the Third Republic when Marshal MacMahon was President. Few monuments have had so chequered a history.

The Place Vendôme nowadays is famous for its fashionable and most expensive hotels. The Ritz is like all other fashionable and expensive hotels, and its most attractive figure is the hall porter, who speaks every language on earth and has much better manners than most princes. The Bristol, where King Edward generally stopped when he was in Paris, had more history and atmosphere. It was here that the Japanese Delegation was housed during the Paris Peace Conference, and where I have seen strange gentlemen of all colours waiting in the hall to consult with the representatives of the nation generally, and perhaps menacingly, regarded as the chief protagonist in the revolt against the domination of the whites.

It might be suggested by the sardonic that the prices at modern hotels, and the fleecing of the traveller, are in accord with the traditions of the Place Vendôme, which was the home, at the height of his splendour, of that amazing financial adventurer, John Law, who during the Regency that followed the death of Louis XIV. became the financial autocrat of France, juggling with paper money and Mississippi shares with such extraordinary deftness that, in 1719, all France was happy and prosperous, and in 1720 all France was unhappy and practically bankrupt.

In a small flat on the Place Vendôme a very beautiful adventuress, who in her time created no little stir in the world, spent the last years of her life in solitude, behind closed shutters and drawn curtains, with all the mirrors carefully covered in order that she might not be horrified by the sight of the wreck of her beauty. She was the Countess Virginie de Castiglione, one of the beauties of the Second Empire, who lived for twenty-nine years after that Empire had come to an end. The Countess was an Italian who made her appearance at the Tuileries in 1855. It is said that she had been one of the many mistresses of Victor Emmanuel, and that she had been sent to Paris by Cavour to attract the Emperor and if possible to persuade him into an alliance with Piedmont against the Austrians. But though Louis-Napoleon had many "indiscretions," the only woman who had any political influence over him was the Empress, and her influence was disastrous. As a matter of fact, Madame de Castiglione's intrigue with Napoleon III. apparently only lasted about a year. She has been described as ambitious without grace, and haughty without reason, a woman infatuated with her own beauty which she was always willing very generously to exhibit. When her beauty faded there was nothing left for her. These are the memories of the Place Vendôme—the pillar whose story is the story of the changing governments of France throughout a century; the Scotch financier to-day the idol of princes and people, to-morrow chased into exile; the brainless old woman hiding behind curtains, ceaselessly mourning her lost beauty; and furtive coloured men in the *foyer* of a modern hotel, waiting to whisper their grievances into the ears of suave statesmen from the Far East.

Chopin died in a house on the Place Vendôme. Ten years before the masterful George Sand had practically kidnapped the Polish composer and dragged him off to Majorca. No man had any chance with George Sand, who first met Chopin at the end of her episode with Alfred de Musset, of which Swinburne wittily said: "Alfred was a terrible flirt and George did not behave as a perfect gentleman." The story of the liaison has been told by them both in two extraordinarily human books, *Confessions d'un enfant du siècle* and *Elle et Lui*. The Abbé Liszt said of George Sand and her lovers: "George Sand catches her butterfly and tames it in her cage by feeding it on flowers and nectar—this is the love period. Then she sticks her pin into it when it struggles—that is the congé, and it always comes from her. Afterwards she vivisects it, stuffs it, and adds it to her collection of heroes for novels."

There was a good deal of the mother in George Sand, and she certainly mothered Chopin whom she first knew when he was a dying man. And it is not without a touch of irony that in his last days he sent to Poland for his sister that he might die in her arms and not in those of the masterful novelist.

I stroll back again to the Opera. The boulevards are streets of cafés and newspaper kiosks. Perhaps the most interesting of the cafés is the Napolitain, on the right-hand side, where English and French journalists used to foregather at a table at which no ordinary French client was ever

PLACE VENDOME.

allowed to sit. Here and there on the Grands Boulevards, between the cafés and the kiosks, are some of the city's most famous theatres, the best-known of which, perhaps, is the Porte St. Martin, where the great Coquelin was rehearsing when he died. I met Coquelin two or three times. He was a kindly, gracious gentleman, with none of the affectations of the stage and with a very wide knowledge of life. He had been one of Gambetta's intimate friends. Coquelin was a Boulonnais, and there is still a French-English journalist living in London who was a schoolfellow of his in Boulogne.

On the right-hand side of the boulevards, down the Rue Vivienne, is the Bourse, as ugly a building as the temple of Mammon should be. The Committee of the London Stock Exchange is very wise in forbidding the public to enter the place where bulls and bears buy and sell. There is a public gallery in the Paris Bourse, and it is a most uncomfortable experience to look down from it and to watch one's fellow-creatures shouting and howling and gesticulating in the excitement of money-making. There is something suggestive in the fact that the Paris Bourse is built on the site of an ancient convent.

The Porte St. Denis and the Porte St. Martin, marking the old gateways of Paris and commemorating two of the saints of France, are pleasant if somewhat incongruous features of the boulevards with their garish modernity, and near them on the north side, rather beyond the limits of fashion, is the Restaurant Marguéry whose founder made a fortune by the invention of *sole Marguéry*. When I knew him he was a very old gentleman with white whiskers and a courtly manner who regularly went from table to table asking his clients if they were being properly served, and treating them as old friends of the family. He sold his restaurant and retired, but the trade dropped so heavily when his presence was no longer there, that he received a large salary to return and continue his gracious enquiries.

The Place de la République is a noisy, ugly open space. Arrived there, the wanderer will probably proceed southward down the Boulevard du Temple to the Place de la Bastille, the site of the famous prison. The taking of the Bastille was the first act of the drama of the Revolution. To the revolutionists, as Carlyle says, "it was tyranny's stronghold." Its fall in 1789 was the end of Bourbonism, but the legend of the Bastille is mainly legend, and despite Dickens and *The Tale of Two Cities* the prison was really a very humane institution, where the aristocrat sent into retirement with a *lettre de cachet* had, as a rule, by no means a bad time.

South of the Place de la République is the district of Paris which used to be called the Marais, the home of high birth and fashion, until in the eighteenth century they migrated across the river to the Faubourg St. Germain. The centre of the district is the Temple which, like the Temple in London, has its name from the fact that it was the headquarters of the Knights Templars. Until the Revolution it was a place of refuge, an Alsatia, and here for a fortnight at the end of 1765, Rousseau stayed in an apartment prepared for him by the Prince de Conti. Though he was proscribed and in danger of arrest, Rousseau was visited by a stream of distinguished callers, including David Hume. "I have visitors of all estates," he wrote, "from the moment I get up to the time I go to bed; I am forced even to dress in public. I have never suffered so much in my life." On August 13, 1792, Louis XVI. and his wife and family were taken to the Temple Prison amid shouts of *Vive la nation*. There he spent four quiet months, giving lessons to his son, playing at draughts, walking in the garden. "He is not of lively feelings," comments Carlyle, "and he is of a devout heart." In January 1793 the king had his last interview in the Temple with Marie Antoinette and his children. He was calm, she was furiously indignant. "*Vous êtes tous des scélérats*," she said as she passed through the anteroom.

The fate of the little Dauphin is still a mystery. He was handed over to the tender mercies of one Simon, a gaoler of the Temple Prison, who, Carlyle says, "taught him to drink and swear and to sing the 'Carmagnole.'" He was brought up in squalor, "his shirt not changed for six months," and it is almost certain that in the Temple he died.

The Temple was entirely pulled down in 1854, and the site is now a market mainly for the sale of gaudy *articles de Paris* and cheap old and new clothing.

The streets of the old Marais in the neighbourhood of the Temple are full of historical interest, and the foreigner,

THE BOURSE

eager to know something of the romance and history of the city in which he is staying, must certainly not neglect the Musée Carnavalet. Among the many famous persons who have dwelt in the district, two in particular appeal to me. One is a quite unknown breeches-maker who, in 1792, wrote the famous revolutionary song the "Carmagnole," that "saucy, rollicking, explosive, diabolic chanson" as it was called, hardly less famous than the "Marseillaise" and which, in a dozen different versions, is always sung when the Parisian is out for trouble. There was an Anarchist version popular twenty years ago in Paris, one verse of which was as follows:

Il y a les sénateurs gâteux,
Il y a les députés véreux,
Il y a les généraux,
Assassins et bourreaux,
Bouchers en uniforme,
Vive le son, vive le son,
Bouchers en uniforme,
Vive le son
D' l'explosion.

I do not suggest that English Socialists should adopt the "Carmagnole," but it is certainly far gayer than their lugubrious "Red Flag."

A greater and far more famous poet, Béranger, lived and died in the street that now bears his name. He also played his part in revolutions, for his song, "Le Vieux Drapeau," was being chanted by the mob when Charles X. was chased from Paris in 1830. The *Vieux Drapeau* was the tricolour of the Revolution and Napoleon, the New Drapeau was the *fleur de lis* reintroduced into France by the Bourbons, the white flag, "*un drapeau*," says the old Napoleonic serjeant, "*que je ne connais pas*." Béranger began life as a waiter in an inn kept by his aunt at Péronne. Coming to Paris he had the usual poet's experience of semi-starvation, at one time only possessing 'three bad shirts which a friendly hand wearied itself in endeavouring to mend," until he found a patron in Lucien Bonaparte. Soon his songs were sung all over France. As Robert Louis Stevenson has said, "He was the only poet of modern times who could altogether have dispensed with printing."

On the border of the Marais is the Place des Vosges where, at number six, is the Musée Victor Hugo. To an apartment in that handsome house the poet with his wife and four children moved from the Rue de Vaugirard in October 1832, and there he stayed until the Revolution of 1848. The Place des Vosges, originally the Place Royale, and during the Revolution the Place de l'Indivisibilité, was laid out by Henri IV., and in a few years became the rival of the Marais as the most fashionable quarter in Paris. In older days the old Palace des Tournelles, the home of the French kings before the building of the Louvre, stood here, and in its courtyard Henri II., the husband of Catherine de Médicis, was killed in a tournament in 1565. Catherine sincerely loved her husband to whom she had been married when she was a girl of fifteen, although he treated her with cold indifference and she had to endure the constant presence of Diane de Poitiers, whose influence with Henri was supreme. In sorrow for the king's death, Catherine demolished the Palais des Tournelles, and the site was for some time used as a horse-market. Catherine lived a widow for twenty-five years, to die the best-hated woman in Europe. " But what could a poor woman have done," Henri IV. once said to one of her critics, " with her husband dead and five little children on her hands, while two families were striving to seize the throne, our own and the Guises? I am astonished that she did not do even worse."

Victor Hugo was thirty when he moved to the Place des Vosges. *Hernani* had been produced at the Théâtre Français three years before, and he had just published *Notre-Dame de Paris* and *Feuilles d'automne*. He was famous and well-to-do, and he filled the rooms in his new home with costly tapestries and fine furniture, some of which he made with his own hands. In the Place des Vosges he began to collect the circle of flatterers which he contrived to retain to the end of his long life. With prosperity had come a certain grossness. " The world and his waistcoat are not wide enough to contain the glory of Victor Hugo or his corpulence," said Théophile Gautier. Mme. Hugo was an odd woman—" a little sallow lady with dark flashing eyes," Dickens described her, devoted to her children, tolerant of her very trying husband, attracted by but certainly not passionately in love with Sainte-Beuve. " I am not loved as I would fain be loved," he confessed; " I dream of love and I have not attained it."

THE PORTE ST. DENIS

Soon after the settlement in the Place des Vosges, Hugo began his liaison with Juliette Drouet, whom he met during the rehearsals of *Lucrezia Borgia* at the Théâtre Porte St. Martin. Their love story is one of the most curious ever written. Juliette was just the ordinary, recklessly extravagant, immoral woman. For ten years at least before she knew the poet she had lived under the protection of one lover after another. Hugo, on the other hand, had hitherto been insensible to the provocative charms of actress and *cocotte*. He described himself as *un homme tranquille et sérieux* and, despite his infatuation for Juliette, her extravagance exasperated him. But soon the greatest of the romantics came to regard Juliette as a sinner who could be saved by love. And he set himself to the task with enthusiasm. His mistress was compelled to live in a small flat with a very small income and without a servant. She was forbidden to go out unless her lover was there to escort her. As the years went on she had to endure the humiliation of knowing that he was constantly unfaithful to her. She was so poor that she sometimes could not afford a fire. She grew fat for want of exercise. And she endured it all, because of her amazing devotion. Right through the period when Hugo lived in the Place des Vosges, Juliette lived this life of a recluse, forbidden to act, poor, lonely, with an occasional treat of a few days in the country with her lover. But the cure was successful, and the courtesan was saved. Rarely even has a poet been loved as Juliette loved Victor Hugo. Her letters are wonderful human documents. In one of them she wrote :

" This is my birthday. You did not even know it—or, rather, I dare say you do not care whether I was ever born or not. Is it true that you do not mind one little bit ? That is all the importance you attach to my love ! And yet one thing is very certain : that I was created and put into the world solely to love you, and God knows with what ardour I fulfil my mission."

In the following year she wrote :

" Farewell, dear soul ; it is impossible to wish an increase of beauty to the man or more glory to the genius ; so, if you are happy, so am I."

And again :

" You failed me again last night, so I shall never count

upon you again. I loved you with all my strength and thought of you even in my sleep. This morning I love you with my whole soul, and heartily long for you, but I know you will not come, so I am cross and sad."

Sometimes she protested. "We are not living in the East, and you have not bought me, thank Heaven." But she soon returned to the note of adoration. I quote from a letter written when the love affair was more than a dozen years old :

"I have just watched you go with inexpressible sadness, my sweet and beautiful beloved. With you have departed the sunshine, the flowers, the pleasant thoughts, the hopes that link past happiness with future bliss."

Juliette died in 1883. The last years of her life were a martyrdom of pain. She had followed Hugo into exile. She had become his never-failing slave, and a few days before her death she wrote :

"Dear adored one, I do not know where I may be this time next year, but I am proud and happy to sign my life-certificate for 1883 with one word : I love you."

Hugo's pockets must have been full of Juliette's letters when he lived in the Place des Vosges. Many of his most charming lyrics were inspired by her love, but her fulsome adulation had the very worst effect on the character of a man notable for colossal conceit.

In the Place des Vosges period Hugo wrote *Ruy Blas*, and was elected to the French Academy and, in 1845, having lost most of his republican fervour and having made friends with Louis-Philippe, whom he had formerly violently attacked, he was created a peer of France. To these years, too, belongs one of his failures, the play called *Les Burgraves*, which caused Balzac to write : "Victor Hugo has never got further than being an *enfant sublime*, and that is all that he ever will be, always the same childish folly of prisons and coffins and a thousand ridiculous absurdities."

It was in the Place des Vosges that Hugo wrote his political testament with its grandiloquent phrases, in which he says of himself : "I am the thinker who is the friend of the toiler ; I am the toiler who is the friend of the thinker." The last year in the Place des Vosges was saddened by the drowning of his daughter Léopoldine, delightfully described as "the freshest and the pearliest of all her father's ballads."

ENTRANCE TO THE PLACE DES VOSGES

When the Revolution of 1848 occurred Victor Hugo had lost much of his prestige. No party was sure of him. Lamartine, a rival poet, was the popular hero. Hugo confessed that he was not even a Republican, and his house was too dangerously near the Rue St. Antoine where so many revolutions have begun. So he moved. There is a rather piquant contemporary description of Mme. Hugo as she was in 1848:

"Madame Victor Hugo is a large woman, with great flamboyant eyes, black arched eyebrows, and a nose audaciously aquiline, lips of an eloquent fulness, a spherical bust, and prominent hips, with crimped and curly locks of ebony straying in every direction, the whole constituting a sort of beauty which, if I were to meet it on a dark night, would make me take to my heels and fly."

This is rather a contrast to Dickens's impression which I have already quoted. The house in which the Hugos lived, by the way, had been the home of Marion Delorme, the mistress of Richelieu, who himself lived in the Place before building the Palais-Cardinal.

The literary associations of the Place des Vosges are not confined to Victor Hugo. At number eleven, Mme. de Sévigné, the greatest of all letter-writers, was born in 1626. All writers of literary letters since Mme. de Sévigné have, says Professor Saintsbury, "imitated her more or less directly, more or less consciously." Her letters supply the intimate history of France in the latter part of the seventeenth century.

Mme. de Sévigné's grandfather was a convert of St. Francis de Sales, while he was in Paris, and the association with the patron-saint of men of letters is interesting. She lived for a while in a house in the Place Royale, as it was then called, after her husband's death in 1651, and before she set up her famous establishment in the Hôtel Carnavalet. While she was there she was within a stone's throw of the house of Ninon de l'Enclos in the Rue des Tournelles. Mme. de Sévigné's husband and son both had affairs with Ninon, her husband wasting a good deal of his wife's money on that fascinating lady—an amazing woman who retained her charm to the end of her days, and had her last love affair when she was eighty!

Ninon remained in the Rue des Tournelles until a few

years before her death, and she entertained there all the wonderful Paris of her time. In her salon, Molière read his *Tartufe* to an assemblage that included Racine, la Fontaine, and the musician Lully, great princes like Condé, and ladies of the real world like Mme. de Sévigné and Mme. Scarron, afterwards Mme. de Maintenon and the solemn wife of the Puritan old age of Louis XIV. Sainte-Beuve says of Ninon de l'Enclos : " She was a living example of vice carried on with intelligence and wit and softened by virtue."

In some of the earlier of her letters Mme. de Sévigné's references to Ninon are naturally caustic, but she never could quite conceal her admiration. In one of them she says : " In spite of her wit, which I will certainly admit is admirable, the thread of insolence that runs through Ninon's conversation is wellnigh insufferable."

After she had moved from the Rue des Tournelles to a house on the Quai facing the Tuileries, de l'Enclos, then well over eighty, had her often-told meeting with Voltaire, who was then seven or eight years old. He was a pupil at the Jesuit College of Clermont, and his father had a flat on the floor above that of the great courtesan. One day their servant let the fire go out and the small boy came down to ask for some red-hot cinders. He found Ninon in the kitchen, for cooking was amongst her accomplishments, making a partridge pasty for lunch, and the acquaintance thus begun resulted in the future philosopher receiving a bequest of two thousand francs with which to begin buying his library.

Many stories are told of Ninon's wit. In her youth the Queen Mother, scandalised by her successes, sent a *lettre de cachet* ordering her to retire into a religious house. But no particular house was mentioned. Ninon read the letter and said to the officer who brought it : " Since the Queen is so good as to leave the choice of a house to me, will you tell her that I select the monastery of the Franciscan monks in Paris." The officer, astounded by her effrontery, had not a word to say, and the Queen thought her answer so funny that she left her alone.

The latter part of the reign of Louis XIV. was an age of great writers, the age of Port Royal and an intense interest in religion—does not Mme. de Sévigné declare that

ST. GERVAIS FROM THE ILE ST. LOUIS

it was *tout propre à inspirer le désir de faire son salut* ?—an age, too, when *monde* and *demi-monde* met on equal, sometimes cordial, terms.

At number thirteen Place des Vosges the great tragédienne Rachel lived at the end of her life, and here after her death in 1858 her clothes and furniture were sold by public auction. Rachel was the daughter of a poor Jewish pedlar, and as a child she and her sister sang in the Paris streets. Seven years after her arrival from the provinces she made her debut at the Théâtre Français. She lives in theatrical history as the creator of *Adrienne Lecouvreur*, a play specially written for her by Legouvé. Rachel had all the instincts of her race for commercial bargaining. Once, so the story goes, she noticed a guitar in the studio of one of her friends. " Give me that guitar," she said, " people will think it is the one with which I earned my living on the Place Royale and on the Place de la Bastille." And as such she afterwards sold it to a dealer for a thousand louis.

Théophile Gautier and Alphonse Daudet both lived at number eight Placc des Vosges. The de Goncourts described Gautier's apartment as " a jumble of odds and ends, like the rooms of an elderly retired actress who has only become possessed of pictures on the bankruptcy of her Italian manager." When Victor Hugo's *Hernani* was first produced Gautier was one of the young enthusiastic romanticists who made the occasion a demonstration against the trammels of the classic tradition, derisively dancing round the bust of Racine in the *foyer* of the Théâtre Français. He must have been an amazing sight in those days, with a great shock of hair and a flaming red waistcoat, worn to *épater la bourgeoisie*. Unlike Hugo, Gautier was entirely uninterested in politics, as he was, Professor Saintsbury reminds us, in religion, morals, science or material progress. He was just an industrious and versatile man of letters, and incidentally a supreme master of French style.

The Place des Vosges is full of Dumas memories. At number six, d'Artagnan visited that terrifying lady, Miladi, the predecessor of the cinema vamp, and it was in the Place that he and the three musketeers met once again in *Twenty Years After*. Much of the action of *La Comtesse de Charny* takes place in the Place.

What a fascinating place of remembrances! Richelieu coming by stealth to visit Marion Delorme; Mme. de Sévigné, a little sad at heart, either at her husband's or her son's philandering with Ninon round the corner; St. Vincent de Paul, who was the director of the nuns at the convent at number seventeen; Hugo, the affectionate husband, with Juliette's last love letters in his pockets; Rachel hurrying to the Théâtre Français; Gautier, Daudet—and d'Artagnan, the greatest immortal of them all.

A short walk westward from the Place des Vosges along the Rue des Francs-Bourgeois and the Rue de Rambuteau, brings the wanderer to the Halles Centrales. A city's markets are always an indication of the character of its people. The Halles Centrales are very much like any other market during the hours when the country carts are delivering their produce and the wholesale buyers are purchasing for their shops. It is in the later hours when madame goes shopping, attended by her neat *bonne*, with the inevitable string bag, that the Paris markets are full of suggestion for the observant foreigner. In England the shopkeeper sells in the way that pleases him best. In France the shopkeeper sells in the way that suits the buyer best. The English butcher, for example, sells as much bone as possible with his meat. The French housewife would decline to buy bone that she did not require, and so the joints are cut to the advantage of the buyer rather than of the seller. In the same way the salad that is bought can all be eaten. Everything, indeed, is done in Paris to make shopping pleasant, and it is all due to the French passion for thrift. In most English households Saturday morning is devoted to buying food for the week. In France the housewife buys each day for the day, and nothing is left over for the next day. If there are cupboards in French flats, they are always bare in the morning.

In 1770 Jean-Jacques Rousseau was permitted to return to Paris with Thérèse le Vasseur, the kitchen wench with whom he had lived for twenty-seven years, and the woman whom Voltaire scornfully described as the *vachine*. They took up their residence near the Halles in the Rue Plastrière, now the Rue Jean-Jacques Rousseau, and Rousseau stayed there until 1778, when he removed to the cottage at

ST. GERVAIS

Ermenonville, where he died. In the Rue Plastrière he finished the *Confessions*, which he had begun in England, and wrote the *Dialogues*.

Jean-Jacques was a bewildering and most unattractive person, an adventurer, content to be the *amant de cœur* of a rich woman ; a touchy, thin-skinned creature who quarrelled with Diderot, with Grimm, with Voltaire, with David Hume ; an ego-maniac eager to appear a worse sinner than he was, and inventing stories of abandoning babes who had never been born. " Rousseau," says Sainte-Beuve, " whenever his diseased self-love and morbid vanity are concerned, has no scruples about lying."

With all this Rousseau is one of the few writers who have had an immediate and direct effect on the history of the world. His influence was infinitely greater than that of Voltaire and all the other eighteenth-century philosophers put together. His *Contrat Social* was the Bible of the French Revolution, and Robespierre was his disciple. And whatever else he was, Rousseau was a great literary artist. Sainte-Beuve says :

" Le jour où il se découvrit tout entier à lui-même, il révéla du même coup à son siècle l'écrivain le plus fait pour exprimer avec nouveauté, avec vigueur, avec une logique mêlée de flamme, les idées confuses qui s'agitaient et qui voulaient naître. Depuis Jean-Jacques c'est dans la forme de langage établie et créée par lui que nos plus grands écrivains ont jeté leurs propres innovations et qu'ils ont tenté de renchérir . . . je n'ai pu indiquer qu'en courant dans l'auteur des *Confessions* les grands côtés par lesquels il demeure un Maître—que saluer le créateur de la rêverie, celui qui nous inocule le sentiment de la nature et le sens de la réalité, le père de la littérature intime et de la peinture intime,—quel dommage que l'orgueil misanthropique s'y mêle ; et que des tons cyniques fassent taches au milieu de tant de beautés charmantes et solides ! "

It is a good and true description—*le père de la littérature intime*. And Mr. Saintsbury has said : " He has achieved absolute perfection in doing what he intended to do. The reader may think that he might have done something else with advantage, but he can hardly think that he could have done this thing better."

La Fontaine was buried in the church of St. Eustache, near the Halles, and Mirabeau's body lay in state there before being carried to the Panthéon.

We turn eastward again, first going south from the Boulevard de Sébastopol to the Rue de Rivoli. Near the Hôtel de Ville, a modern building finished in 1883, the old town hall with its wealth of historic interest having been destroyed during the troubles of 1871, is the great church of St. Gervais. It is dedicated to the two brothers, Gervasius and Protarius, martyred in Rome by Nero, whose bones were brought to Paris by St. Germain. In 1652 the poet Scarron, a sick man of forty-two, who gained an exiguous living by writing the witty Mazarinades at the expense of the Cardinal, was married to Françoise d'Aubigné, a girl of seventeen. Françoise had had a hard childhood, and for her there was no choice but the poet Scarron or a convent. Her father was a conscienceless adventurer, the son of one of the fiercest of the Huguenot leaders, always in trouble with the authorities. He had been married in a prison and his daughter was born in a prison, her mother never showing her the smallest affection. But Françoise had inherited her grandfather's character, his strength and his sternness, and pitiful as were her beginnings, she was to live to be Mme. de Maintenon, wife of the King of France.

Still going eastward the wanderer is back again on the Place de la Bastille and the Faubourg St. Antoine which, far more than Montmartre, far more than the Quartier Latin, has been the birthplace of revolution and *émeutes*, probably because it is the home of ugliness and poverty, and consequently of discontent. It was in the Faubourg St. Antoine that the Defarges had their wine-shop in Dickens's *Tale of Two Cities*. I quote the English novelist's description of the Faubourg as it was at the end of the eighteenth century :

" The darkness of it was heavy—cold, dirt, sickness, ignorance, and want were the lords in waiting on the saintly presence—nobles of great power all of them ; but, most especially the last. Samples of a people that had undergone a terrible grinding and regrinding in the mill, and certainly not in the fabulous mill which ground old people young, shivered at every corner, passed in and out

ST. PAUL

at every doorway, looked from every window, fluttered in every vestige of a garment that the wind shook. The mill which had worked them down was the mill that grinds young people old ; the children had ancient faces and grave voices ; and upon them, and upon the grown faces, and ploughed into every furrow of age and coming up afresh was the sign, Hunger."

Beyond the Place de la Nation and of course outside the city boundary is the Bois de Vincennes, little known to the tourist, but with the charm that belongs to all the woods with which Paris is surrounded. There was a royal Château at Vincennes before the Revolution, a château sometimes used as a prison. Here the great Henri IV. was imprisoned in 1574 for plotting with his wretched brother-in-law d'Alençon against Charles IX. and the Queen Mother, Catherine de Médicis. His imprisonment was neither long nor onerous, Henri obtaining pardon, partly through an admirable defence drawn up by his wife, Marguerite de Valois, and partly by showing appropriate penitence. In his interview with Catherine de Médicis " he wept most piteously, shedding hot tears for his innocence." He was not innocent, but Henri of Navarre was an admirable actor.

Diderot, the philosopher, was imprisoned in Vincennes in 1749 after the publication of his pamphlet, *Lettre sur les aveugles*, and it was during this imprisonment that he began to plan the great Encyclopædia. A few years later, in 1777, Mirabeau was imprisoned at Vincennes by a *lettre de cachet*. His offence was an elopement with another man's wife. He spent his three and a half years in a characteristic way, writing extraordinarily obscene letters, and compiling a series of valuable political treatises on *lettres de cachet*. All the great figures of the French Revolution have been coloured for us by the genius of Carlyle, and to Carlyle Mirabeau was " a tempestuous volcano of a man, the aristocratic forerunner of Danton." As a matter of fact he was a great political philosopher who might have guided France from autocracy to Parliamentarianism if Marie Antoinette had been less obstinate and Louis XVI. less stupid. He was also a typical Frenchman of his own sceptical age. During his visit to England he shocked the highly conscientious Whig, Sir Samuel Romilly, by declaring that there were often occasions when *la petite morale était ennemi de la grande*.

The Place de la Nation was the Place du Trône until the Revolution, when it was ironically renamed La Place du Trône Renversé. One thousand three hundred and forty men and women were guillotined on the Place de la Nation during the Terror, the most distinguished of them being the poet André Chénier, whose verse was the one important contribution to French literature in the long period between Voltaire and Hugo. Chénier was half a Greek and was born in Constantinople in 1762,—the naturalised Greek, by the way, is an interesting figure in the history of French literature, the poet Moréas being perhaps the most notable of the later Franco-Greek writers. Chénier was in London in 1787 as secretary to the French Ambassador, and it is sometimes said that as a poet he was influenced by Milton and Thomson. But he hated England —*nation toute à vendre à qui peut la payer*—and he went back in 1790 to the Paris of the early days of the Revolution. Chénier was as keen a politician as Lamartine in the next century. He was a fervent Constitutionalist, writing an ode to Charlotte Corday, in which he congratulated France that thanks to her *un scélérat de moins rampe dans cette fange*. Thanks to his brother, who was a member of the Convention, he managed to escape arrest for some time, living in seclusion in Versailles, but he fell into the hands of the Terrorists on March 7, 1794, and was guillotined on July 25, one of the very last of Robespierre's victims. Chénier has been described by no less authority than Sainte-Beuve as the first of the French Romantics. As a matter of fact, he was the last of the Classicists. To Hugo and his fellows a poet was *une force qui va*, to Chénier a poet was *une abeille industrieuse*. Chénier, the poet, was in every way the child of the age of the philosophers. He shared their faith that the world could be saved by knowledge :

> Souvent mon vol, armé des ailes du Buffon,
> Franchit avec Lucrèce, au flambeau de Newton,
> La ceinture d'azur sur le globe étendue.

REBUILDING PONT TOURNELLE

X

MONTMARTRE

THE hill of Montmartre is reached from the Boulevard by way of the Rue de la Chaussée d'Antin, and thence by the Rue Blanche or the Rue Pigalle, or by way of the Rue Laffitte and the Rue des Martyrs. Mme. Récamier, whom Napoleon hated and who nursed Chateaubriand in his old age, lived in the Rue de la Chaussée d'Antin ; so did Mme. Roland, the beautiful Girondist, " serene and queenly," and Mme. Necker, the mother of Mme. de Staël, and Gibbon of *The Decline and Fall*, who nearly married Mme. Necker. The world may rejoice that the plan was frustrated, for had it matured, there would certainly have been no Mme. de Staël. It is impossible to conceive such a woman with Gibbon as father. In the Rue de la Chaussée d'Antin there lived an even more famous person, Baron Danglars, one of the villains of *Monte Cristo*, the banker whom Monte Cristo contrived to ruin, and near by in a parallel street, the Rue du Helder, was " the large and fashionable dwelling " of Fernand Mondégo and his wife, the beautiful Mercédès, to whom Monte Cristo, then Edmond Dantès, was affianced when he was arrested and taken to the Château d'If. Mirabeau died in the Rue de la Chaussée d'Antin in 1791, already grown fearful of the Revolution which he had done so much to bring about. The spring sun shone into his room on the day of his death, and almost his last words were, " *Si ce n'est pas là Dieu c'est du moins son cousin germain*." At a house in this street Napoleon met Joséphine de Beauharnais for the first time.

The Rue Meyerbeer, a comparatively new street, now runs from the Rue Chaussée d'Antin to the Opera House.

Meyerbeer, a German Jew, born in Berlin, was one of the many foreign artists to whom Paris has given fortune and fame. His *Robert le Diable* was produced in the thirties of last century when the Opera House was in the Rue Le Peletier. It is said that the composer could never quite believe that he had made a great success, and that he went every morning to look at the bills outside the Opera House, to see whether *Robert le Diable* was to be performed. When it was, in sheer joy he emptied his pockets to the loafers in the street. The consequence was that whenever a Meyerbeer opera was played in the evening, the Rue Le Peletier was simply swarming with beggars in the morning.

At the top of the Rue de la Chaussée d'Antin is the Place de la Trinité, from which three streets run northward to the Boulevard de Clichy and Montmartre. On the left hand of these three streets is the Rue de Clichy. Turning off it on the right is the Rue de Bruxelles where Zola died. In common with many of the great French writers of the nineteenth century Zola was a sad, sombre figure of a man. In his youth the de Goncourts described him as " restless, anxious, profound, complicated, reserved and not easily understood." He worked almost as hard as Daudet to earn a living, declaring in his early days that his one compensation was good food. " When I have not something good at dinner I am unhappy, quite unhappy. It is the only thing : other things do not exist as far as I am concerned." He was sometimes so impecunious that he had to pawn his coat and trousers and stay at home working in his shirt. Zola was the disciple of Flaubert, and like Flaubert he was by nature a romanticist who compelled himself to be a realist. Émile Faguet says that he had a " coarsening vision which made him remember things seen not exactly as they were, but larger, more highly coloured, more formidable." He was a great collector of facts, and when he had his facts he was as romantic in coarsening them as other writers are in sentimentalising them. It is amusing in thinking of Zola as a hunter of the realities—if possible the unpleasant realities—to recall a description of him in the de Goncourt *Journal* :

" Zola's nose is quite peculiar ; it is a nose which interrogates, approves, condemns ; a nose which is sad or

MONTMARTRE

gay ; a nose which is inhabited by its master's physiognomy : a real hunting-dog's nose, which impressions, sensations and desires divide at the end into two little lobes which seem to twitch at moments."

Zola has been described by Sir Edmund Gosse as " a thunderer or bellower on the trumpet," but, as Sir Edmund has pointed out, he " can sometimes breathe through silver, particularly in his short stories, which are very little known in England." That he was a man of splendid courage and fine sympathy was shown in his fight for Dreyfus, the not very attractive victim of what is still to foreigners an incomprehensible political plot.

The streets on the way to Montmartre are peopled with literary, artistic, musical and theatrical ghosts. Eastward of the Rue de Bruxelles at the junction of the Avenue Trudaine and the Rue des Martyrs is the restaurant in which Fragson, the famous Anglo-French comedian, dined before going back to his flat to be murdered by his father, and a little south in the Rue St. Georges, the composer Auber died. Auber never, if he could possibly help it, took off his hat. He composed with his hat on, he ate with his hat on, and if he went to the theatre he insisted on having a box in order that he need not take his hat off. Indeed, although he was not a Jew, he went to the Synagogue for the same reason, and would never go into a church.

In the Rue de Douai the great Russian novelist, Turgenev, lived during his long stay in France. Edmond de Goncourt met him one night at dinner at Gustave Flaubert's, Théophile Gautier being the other guest. The wise adventurer in Paris always, by the way, has a copy of the *Journal* in his pocket. De Goncourt says :

" Turgenev, the delightful giant, the lovable barbarian, whose white hairs fall down on to his eyes, with a deep fold that runs across his forehead from one temple to the other like a furrow, with his infantile speech, charms us from the soup onwards by that mixture of simplicity and depth which makes the Slav race so seductive—emphasised in his case by the originality of his mind and by his immense and cosmopolitan knowledge.

" He told us about the month he spent in prison after the publication of *A Sportsman's Sketches* ; of that month when he had, for his cell, the archives of the police of his district, of which he read through the secret files. He described to us, with the detail of a painter and a novelist, the police inspector who one day, intoxicated by Turgenev's champagne, said to him, touching his elbow and lifting his glass into the air : 'To Robespierre.'" Then he stopped for a moment, lost in his reflections, and began again : "If I took pride in these things, I should ask that on my tombstone should be carved what my book did for the emancipation of the serfs—and nothing more. Yes, I should only ask that. . . . The Emperor Alexander had me informed that the reading of my book was one of the principal motives of his determination."

In the early part of his life Gounod lived in this Quartier, in the Rue Rochechouart. As might be supposed of a man who composed masses as well as operas, Gounod had intermittent spasms of religious enthusiasm. During one of them he became very anxious to secure the conversion of Sarah Bernhardt. He went, so it is said, to her flat in the Boulevard Pereire, near the Porte Maillot, and implored, persuaded and wept. The great Sarah remained silent until the composer had finished, and then very decisively remarked, *Non, moi je reste athéiste*.

The Boulevard de Clichy and the streets reaching to it from the south are the home of the night restaurant and the cabaret. The night restaurants of Montmartre, together with such bizarre vulgarities as le Ciel, l'Enfer, and the rest, largely exist on foreign custom, for, as I have said, the real Paris is early to bed and early to rise. Some of the cabarets, too, openly cater for the Puritan's craving for the nasty when he once gets out of his own country. But none the less there is very genuine and distinctive art in the Montmartre cabaret. The songs would hardly meet with the approval of the Bradford Watch Committee, but they have wit, they are often ironic and they are sometimes most admirable satire. Fashion in cabarets changes almost from month to month. The best of them was once the Chat Noir. More recently the best was unquestionably La Lune Rousse where my friend, Lucien Boyer, a most admirable poet, used to appear every night. M. Boyer's quality may be judged from his "Gerbe de Tommy," taken from his *Chansons des Poilus* :

A MONTMARTRE SQUARE

En mil-neuf-cent-quinze, à Rouen. . . . Sous un ciel blême :
Devant une fleuriste un Tommy s'arrêta.
Sans doute, il veut des fleurs pour la femme qu'il aime,
Pensa-t-elle en voyant son air un peu bêta.

De tous ses mimosas elle fit une gerbe :
Plus elle en ajoutait plus il criait : " Encor ! "
Et Tommy repartit flegmatique, superbe,
Portant son mimosa comme un panache d'or.

On disait : Ces Anglais vraiment font des folies !
Les femmes chuchotaient : Dame, c'est le printemps,
Et dans notre pays les filles sont jolies
Et ce galant Tommy n'a pas plus de vingt ans.

C'est égal, tant de fleurs pour une demoiselle,
C'est trop, c'est beaucoup trop, c'en est prétentieux !
Il faut qu'elle soit belle, impértinemment belle,
Car pour une princesse on ne ferait pas mieux.

Enfin, chaque passant trouvait un mot à dire,
Mais le petit Tommy par son rêve conduit,
Passait indifférent avec un doux sourire
Et la gerbe d'amour qu'il serrait contre lui.

Place du Vieux-Marché, Tommy, la tête nue
Comme les gentlemen qu'on voit dans Hyde-Park,
Simplement s'arrêta devant une statue
Et déposa la gerbe aux pieds de Jeanne d'Arc.

I have a delightful memory of Lucien Boyer in a Montmartre restaurant lunching on eggs and bacon as a delicate compliment to my nationality, and writing a poem on the back of the menu while he ate and talked.

North of the Boulevard de Clichy the streets are uncomfortably steep till one reaches the hill-top and the Sacré Cœur, and the elderly and the wise complete the journey on the funicular railway. For the Sacré Cœur I have no affection, but for the small restaurants, or at least one or two of them near by, where one eats in the open air to be enthralled by a panorama of Paris in the valley below, I have a deep love. I am not indeed sure that an evening so spent is not the best that Paris has to offer. Did not one famous Montmartrois say : " *Maintenant en guise d'apéritif, je vais vous offrir une vue splendide sur Paris. C'est tout que je possède.*"

The Sacré Cœur is size and very little else. It was built after the war of 1870 by a France, thanks to defeat, *humiliée et repentante*, and unattractive as it is, it is a church dominating a great city. The Sacré Cœur stands for a rather sentimental Catholicism which is a striking contrast to the intellectual Catholicism of such a church as St. Sulpice.

On the west slope of the hill of Montmartre is the Cimetière du Nord where Heine is buried and Henri Mürger, the author of *La Vie de Bohème*, and the two uncomfortable brothers de Goncourt, and Théophile Gautier, and Renan, the ex-monk.

Montmartre has played its part in all the revolutions. Just before the Commune it was said that at Montmartre "insurrection held its guns and its drums always ready," and it was the seizing of the cannons at Montmartre that began the outbreak of 1871. M. Clemenceau was Mayor of Montmartre in those days, and being a realistic politician was opposed to the sentimental adventure of the Communists. "Half accomplice, half dupe of M. Thiers," is a Communist description of Clemenceau then.

WASH-HOUSES ON THE SEINE

XI

OUTSIDE THE CITY WALLS

THE joy of Paris in the summer is the woods that surround it. It is indeed not a city set upon a hill, but a city set, as it were, in the middle of a forest. Of all the woods of Paris the Bois de Boulogne is the best known, though it is by no means the most beautiful. It contains admirable and most expensive restaurants, two race-courses where it is possible to see racing cheaply and without being deafened by the shouting of Hebraic bookmakers, two lakes, a waterfall, and innumerable shady walks. Here of a morning Parisian " hig lif " disports itself on horseback and in motors, and here, a far more interesting sight, M. Jacques Bonhomme comes on a Sunday afternoon with his wife and family, a tremendous figure of enthusiasm. Jacques Bonhomme is generally well in the forties, for he belongs to a prudent tribe that deprecates early ill-considered marriages. He is immensely good-humoured, and he plays with his small children with an abandon that few Englishmen could imitate. There is still a curious legend in England that in French there is no word for home. Not so many years ago a distinguished English novelist declared in one of his stories that every man you meet in the Paris streets is either going to his mistress or coming from her. The truth is that the French are an intensely domestic people, respecting family ties and family obligations in a way hardly realised in England. Let the Bois de Boulogne on a Sunday afternoon witness if I lie.

It is through the Bois de Boulogne, if haply one has a motor, or can hire one, that one makes one's way to St. Cloud, lunching may be at the Pavillon Bleu, built by the side of the river, and walking afterwards into the park.

It was at St. Cloud on August 1, 1589, that Henri III., the last and worst of the Valois, was stabbed to death by a crazy monk called Clement. Henri had been compelled to leave Paris by the plots of the League and was camping at St. Cloud, waiting for the arrival of Henri of Navarre to attempt the recapture of the city. Hatred was the main factor of his life. He hated the Guises and he hated his mother, Catherine de Médicis, and it was his hatred of her which caused him with his last breath to name Navarre as his successor.

In those days what afterwards became the famous Château of St. Cloud was the country-house of the Archbishop of Paris. In the middle of the seventeenth century it was bought by the Duc d'Orléans, the brother of Louis XIV., and it was the home of his second wife, the *Madame* of the de Maintenon period, a stumpy, red-faced little German princess who had an intense love for her dogs and a senseless hatred of the King's mentor. The Duc d'Orléans died at St. Cloud fourteen years before his brother, and it was in the palace that his son, the Regent, received Peter the Great when he came to western Europe to astonish and be astonished.

At the *coup d'État* of the 18th Brumaire (1799) Napoleon insisted that the Council of Ancients should adjourn from thc Tuileries to the Château of St. Cloud, the plot being ingeniously carried through by his brother, Lucien, who called various members of the Assembly to meet at different times. The resignation of Barras, the chief member of the Directoire, was announced, but the majority of the députés was unwilling to accept the new dictator. When Napoleon arrived with a body of grenadiers he was greeted with loud cries of "Long live the Republic, down with the Dictator," whereupon Murat rushed into the hall like another Cromwell and drove out the representatives. At ten o'clock that night a rump of the body met again and created the Consulate, and as Bourrienne records: "By three o'clock in the morning the palace of St. Cloud had resumed its accustomed calm."

The Concordat which re-established the Catholic religion in France was signed on July 15, 1801, and became law in the following April. For a long time his advisers vainly urged Napoleon himself to hear mass, and at last

GARDENS AT ST. CLOUD

he consented, and mass was said in a small room at St. Cloud opening out of his study. "The apartment," says Bourrienne, "was used during the week as a bathroom, and on Sunday a portable altar was fixed up, the door of communication was opened and mass, which never took more than twelve minutes, was said while Napoleon was reading memoranda at his desk." Napoleon was first addressed as "Sire" at St. Cloud and begged by Cambacérès to proclaim himself Emperor. His reply was characteristic of a man, on occasion, colossal in hypocrisy: "All that can contribute to the welfare of the country is essential to my happiness. I accept the title which you believe to be useful for the glory of the nation. I submit to the sanction of the people the law of hereditary succession. I hope that France will never repent the honour with which she may surround my family, but at all events my spirit will not be with my posterity when they cease to merit the love and confidence of a great nation."

Charles X., the last of the Bourbons, less able than any of them either to learn or forget, issued the ordinances that cost him his throne from St. Cloud. He had himself crowned at Rheims on the death of his brother, Louis XVIII., and from the beginning of his reign he made it clear that there was to be no compromise with a Liberalism detestable to Bourbon traditions. "I would rather hew wood," he said, "than be a king like the King of England." The Government that he set up was scornfully described by the Duke of Wellington as "a Government by priests, through priests, for priests." Early in 1830 news came to France of the capture of Algiers by the French fleet, and this seemed to Charles to be the moment for dissolving the Chamber, suppressing the free press and generally curbing "the turbulent Democracy which has invaded even our laws and tends to displace legitimate power." Charles was an old gentleman of seventy-three, and he appears to have been considerably astonished when Paris rose and he was obliged hurriedly to depart from St. Cloud, first to Versailles, and then to England, the home of so many *rois français en exil.*

St. Cloud was an imperial residence during the Second Empire, a quiet country-house where Napoleon and Eugénie stayed in comparative privacy impossible at the Tuileries or at Compiègne, where most of their theatrical parties were given. Here of an evening, so Augustin Filon relates, Prosper Mérimée, the author of *Carmen*, who had been a friend of Eugénie and her mother in Spain, would sit and read his latest manuscript to the Empress and her ladies.

In 1855, when Queen Victoria paid her visit to Paris, rooms were prepared for her and the Prince Consort and their children in the Palace of St. Cloud, and one wonders whether, installed in an apartment arranged to resemble the domesticity of Windsor, Victoria dreamed of the other great historical personages, so extraordinarily unlike her, who had slept in the palace in other days.

It was at St. Cloud on the morning of July 15, 1870, that the Council was held which decided on war with Germany, Lebœuf assuring the Emperor that the French army was ready to the buttons on its gaiters and that victory was certain. Émile Ollivier, the Prime Minister, drove straight from St. Cloud to the Chamber to make his famous declaration: "*De ce jour commence pour les Ministres, mes collègues, et pour moi une grande responsabilité. Nous l'acceptons le cœur léger.*" That evening the streets of Paris were filled with a mob shouting "*A Berlin, à Berlin.*"

It was a dull grey morning when Napoleon left St. Cloud for the last time. He had a short consultation with his ministers, gravely said good-bye to all the suite and drove to the station with his wife and son. As the train started the Empress called out to the Prince Imperial, who accompanied his father, "*Louis, fais bien ton devoir.*" That was on July 29. On August 2 a telegram came to St. Cloud from the Emperor announcing what proved to be the inconsiderable victory at Saarbruck. It ran: "Louis has just received his baptism of fire, his coolness was admirable, he was as unconcerned as if he had been strolling in the Bois de Boulogne." And then followed news of disaster after disaster. "Our troops," ran one telegram, "are in full retreat, nothing must be thought of now beyond the defence of the capital." The Empress was told the fatal news at half-past eleven at night, and for once rising to something like greatness, she said: "The Dynasty is lost, we must think only of France"; adding to a lady who offered her sympathy, "No sentiment, I implore you, I need all my courage." At half-past two in the morning she left St. Cloud for the Tuileries.

On October 18, William, the old King of Prussia, stood in the gardens of St. Cloud with Bismarck and Von Moltke, looking over Paris, picking out the Invalides, Notre-Dame, the Arc de Triomphe, and perhaps thinking, like another Blücher, what a city it was to sack. During the bombardment the palace was set on fire and totally destroyed, the French say by the Germans, the Germans by the French, one German writer sententiously exclaiming as he records the loss, "How the French rage against their own flesh!"

I have pleasant recollections of St. Germain-en-Laye, its château and its forest. I have stood many times on the famous *terrasse* looking over the valley of the Seine with the spires of Paris in the distance. I have drunk most admirable Vouvray *tête* in a restaurant on the cobbled square opposite the château. I was present in the château itself, now a museum, when the Peace Treaty terms were handed to the Austrian delegates, and a very moving speech of protest from one of them was interrupted by a photographer falling through one of the specimen cases fixed against the wall.

The first Château of St. Germain was built on the site of an ancient monastery in the twelfth century, and entirely rebuilt by François I. During the reigns of the Valois kings the Court was frequently at St. Germain, and Henri IV. finished what is called the New Château, where Louis XIV. spent a great deal of his time before Versailles became his principal residence. At St. Germain James II. of England found shelter when he fled from London with his queen, Mary of Modena, and his baby son, the unlucky prince who lives in history as the "Old Pretender." They lived at St. Germain until James's death in 1701. There is nothing finer in all the long reign of Louis XIV. than his kindness to his exiled brother of England. His reign had passed its zenith, William of Orange was a formidable enemy with whom it had become good policy for France to be at peace, but no question of political expediency could tempt the French king to desert his friend, and he showed amazing patience with the futilities of the exiled Stuart.

When Queen Mary of England died in 1694 a request came from St. Germain to Versailles that the French Court should wear no mourning. The order was obeyed, says Saint-Simon, but people thought this kind of revenge rather petty. In 1697 the Duke of Portland was sent to France to endeavour to arrange an understanding, and particularly to suggest that William's friendship could be secured if King James and his family were removed from St. Germain. But the Ambassador was warned not to mention the subject to Louis. I quote Saint-Simon :

" The King would not only refuse positively to change his decision, but would be highly offended if he heard a word on the subject. He assured Portland that the King was ready to reciprocate the friendly advances of the King of England, but a single word about St. Germain would spoil everything."

The constant kindness and consideration are the more remarkable since Louis had no illusions about James's capacity or his chances of recovering his throne. Writing in 1694 he said : " The best thing King James can do is to forget that he has ever been King of England."

St. Germain was the scene of constant Jacobite intrigues in the last ten years of the seventeenth century. There was hardly a politician in England who had sworn fealty to William who was not negotiating with James, making the best of both kings, if not of both worlds. In the town of St. Germain itself there lived an army of spies in William's employ, watching the visitors who entered the château. They, when they were cautious, were carried inside the gates in curtained sedan-chairs to avoid " the curious persons and knaves and spies, and the former as dangerous as the latter, but not designedly."

James had a paralytic seizure in April 1701, and Louis at once ordered that he should take the waters at Bourbon. " The King was very liberal in providing everything they wanted, and, though they used to travel without ceremony, gave orders that they should be treated everywhere with the same honours as were given to himself." The visit to Bourbon had no beneficial effect, and in September James had another stroke which left no hope of his recovery. The King, Mme. de Maintenon and all the French royal family frequently drove from Versailles to St. Germain to see the dying King, and on September 13 Louis assured him that he would recognise his son as King of England, Scotland

and Ireland, another generous action which Saint-Simon properly says was extremely bad politics. Before he died, James gave his last admonition to his son: "Be a good Catholic, fear God, obey your mother next after God. Be entirely dependent on the King of France." This last piece of advice was hardly likely to make the prince popular in England.

Immediately after his father's death the young prince received the homage of the St. Germain courtiers and was proclaimed James III., King of England, Scotland and Ireland, at the palace gates. Saint-Simon was not alone in his criticisms of this procedure, which was recognised by every one who was not a sentimentalist as calculated vastly to strengthen the position of William of Orange. In 1708 the Old Pretender left St. Germain to join the abortive expedition for the invasion of Scotland. When he arrived at Dunkirk it was discovered that he was suffering from measles and this delayed the start. When at last he was well enough to embark a furious storm was raging off Ostend and the expedition was obliged to return. Before he left France, Louis had given him a sealed packet which contained his patent as a Marshal of France. "It would be difficult," says Saint-Simon, "to become one on easier terms." It was on this occasion that the prince used for the first time the title Chevalier de St. Georges. Saint-Simon says of him: "He showed plenty of courage and determination, but they were rendered fruitless by the effects of his bad education, which had been narrow and austere. The Queen, his mother, had brought him up in this manner, partly from a mistaken view of religion, partly to keep him in subjection and dependence on herself for, with all her piety, she was fond of domineering."

Fénelon, certainly no sycophant, described him as having "a quick apprehension of truth, a sincere love of it, a perfect relish of that divine fortitude which is founded upon submission to Providence." It was pitiful that a prince of such good parts should have been fated to a life so ineffective and so full of failure.

After the death of Louis XIV. the position of the exiles in St. Germain became much more uncomfortable. The Regent's policy was to be on good terms with the English Government, and the presence of Mary of Modena and her children at St. Germain was a considerable nuisance. After the tragic failure of 1715, thanks to the Jacobite loyalty that never failed, the prince contrived to return to France, and went to St. Germain to say good-bye to his mother, and four years afterwards he took up his residence in Rome, where he lived for fifty years, and where his son, the Young Pretender, was born. James has been badly maligned by Thackeray, who frequently spoke evil of dignitaries without due cause. He may have been in his old age, as a witty Frenchman described him *un dévot à l'excès*, but he was high-principled and dignified. He lies in St. Peter's under a magnificent monument, the work of Canova, which many a successful dead king might envy. With the death of Mary of Modena in 1718 the connection of the Stuarts with the Château of St. Germain came to an end.

There are frequent references to St. Germain-en-Laye in the Dumas romances, particularly in *Marguerite de Valois* and *Vingt Ans après*. The novelist's description of the flight of Anne of Austria and her son Louis XIV. from Paris to the Château of St. Germain, thanks to the fidelity of d'Artagnan, will be particularly remembered. Near St. Germain Dumas built his Châtelet du Monte Cristo, and for a short time lived a life of gorgeous extravagance. So popular was he that it is said that the receipts of the Compagnie du Chemin de Fer de l'Ouest, then in its infancy, increased by twenty thousand francs a year owing to the number of people who were curious to see the great novelist's royal residence. He brought down the Company from the Comédie-Française to play his pieces in the local theatre for the benefit of the poor, and afterwards had firework displays on the *terrasse* and supper-parties in all the hotels. Louis-Philippe rejoiced at the prosperity of St. Germain and wished that Versailles might also become gay and popular. "Well, Sire," said one of his ministers, "Alexandre Dumas has lately been sentenced to a fortnight's imprisonment for neglecting his duty in the National Guards; make an order for him to spend the fortnight in Versailles, and I guarantee your Majesty that Versailles will be lively enough."

Oddly enough Dumas had Parliamentary ambitions and stood as candidate for St. Germain, but the electors rejected him because they did not consider him sufficiently moral to be their representative. His generosity was unbounded, and although he spent every penny he earned, he spent little of it on himself. "My biographer," he once said, "will not fail to point out that I was a basket with holes in it, forgetting, of course, to mention that, as a rule, it was not I who made the holes."

XII

VERSAILLES

THE story of the Palace of Versailles begins with a visit paid by Louis XIV., then a young man of twenty-three, to his Minister of Finance, Nicolas Fouquet, at his wonderful country-house at Vaux. It was never wise for the minister of an autocrat to build himself too gorgeous a palace. Hampton Court had not a little to do with the fall of Wolsey ; Vaux was the undoing of Fouquet, an astute man of figures who had looked after the considerable fortune of Mazarin, and in collecting the national taxes had not forgotten himself. Fouquet was " a friend of the arts, a friend of letters, a friend of women," the patron of La Fontaine and Corneille, and a man whom Mme. de Sévigné found witty. The palace at Vaux had cost Fouquet eighteen million francs. Three villages had been destroyed in order that its gardens might be spacious. And Louis, young, arrogant, hating the idea that any one should possess anything finer than his own possessions, was filled with envy. His own country-houses at Fontainebleau and St. Germain were mere villas compared to Fouquet's palace, and it was intolerable that a subject should be better housed than his master. To envy was added anger when he discovered that his host possessed a picture of Louise de la Vallière. Sour-faced Colbert, who hated Fouquet and wanted his place, was ready at the King's elbow to whisper into his willing ear that such a fortune could only have been accumulated by robbing the royal revenues. And a month after the visit, d'Artagnan arrested Fouquet, Louis took over his architect, Le Vau, and his gardener, Le Nôtre, and appropriated his orange trees. With architect, gardener and orange trees in hand, he began to build the palace of

VERSAILLES

Versailles and to lay out its grounds, building on to a hunting-box to which his father had often gone to escape from Richelieu and the cares of State.

Versailles plays a great part in the history of France, and not a small part in the history of Europe. In the eighteenth century its splendours were shoddily imitated by every petty German princeling. It set the pace for European royalty, and it was a pace that killed.

It was at Fontainebleau that Louis first met Louise de la Vallière. She was then a girl of seventeen. Claude Ferval, who has written her story so well, a story that the poet Jean Richepin has described as "so romantic, so unreal, so improbable," says that the girl was "more than pretty, with her tender appealing eyes, her frank mouth and her fair silvery hair, and she had a certain air of modesty and honesty which made her respected as well as desired." There is no question that Louise loved the King sincerely and passionately. She was always disinterested and hardly ever happy. She was the central figure, Queen and Queen Mother being hardly regarded, in the first series of fêtes that Louis gave at Versailles in 1664. Remembering Ariosto, the master of the revels had conceived an enchanted island that had contrived to float to France. On the first night the knights of Ariosto, magnificently dressed, paraded before the ladies of the Court.

"The King, representing Roger, mounted one of the finest horses in the world, whose flame-coloured harness shone with gold and silver, and precious stones. The King, like all the members of his troop, was armed in the Greek fashion, and wore a cuirass plated with silver and covered with rich embroidery in gold and diamonds. His bearing and all his gestures were worthy of his rank: his helmet, covered with flame-coloured plumes, was worn with incomparable grace; and never did a bolder or a more soldierly air make a mortal superior to other men."

Then as night fell there was a procession of the seasons and pagan gods, Lulli leading the music and Molière appearing as Pan. On the second night Molière and his troupe performed his comedy, *La Princesse d'Elis*, the performance concluding with a ballet of fauns and shepherds "so grand, so full of incident and so agreeable that nothing finer in the way of a ballet has ever been seen." Fireworks that apparently rivalled the achievements of Mr. Brock were the *pièce de résistance* of the third night, and after dinner the ladies drew lots for "jewellery, ornaments, silver and other similar things," it being arranged that La Vallière should win a beautiful bracelet greatly envied by the King's sister-in-law. In 1664, however, the palace was still only a comparatively small house, and the courtiers loudly grumbled since, when the festivities were over, many of them had scarcely a hole in which to take shelter.

In the next year Henrietta Maria, wife of Charles I., stopped for five days at Versailles, and the first performance of Molière's *L'Amour médecin* took place in the palace. La Vallière was created a duchess in 1666, but already her long expiation had begun. Françoise Athenaïs de Tonnay Charente, Marquise de Montespan, had arrived at Versailles, "beautiful as the day," to quote Saint-Simon, witty, ambitious, shameless, and, when he met her, Louis began to grow indifferent to the timid charms of Louise. The courtiers, after their manner, were quick to note the passing of one favourite and the rising of another, and a verse was handed from hand to hand in the salons and corridors of the palace :

On dit que La Vallière
S'en va sur son déclin ;
Montespan prend sa place,
Il faut que tout y passe
Ainsi de main en main.

La Vallière, although she was only just over twenty, was already losing her beauty. Her manner was sad, her eyes were often filled with tears. De Montespan was a figure of love and laughter, determined to win the King's favour, consulting, so it is said, sorcerers to gain her end. Whether or not the sorcery was effective, her conquest of the King was complete. With almost incredible cruelty he compelled La Vallière to remain at Versailles to watch her rival's triumph and in a sort of queer way to cover the King's inconstancy. Claude Ferval has written a vivid picture of de Montespan :

"She flaunted her glories but failed to charm any one. She was full of greed and ambition and caprice, but no real love, none of that blushing weakness which wins affection and asks forgiveness. An incomparable carnal splendour, an inextinguishable laugh, a richness of blood which rendered the use of rouge on her cheeks unnecessary, all added to the scandal rather than excused it. The opulence of her arms and hair, full of precious stones, seemed to court admiration rather than love. But as she was, the King idolised his new mistress and the Court was at her feet. It is true that no one was more amusing than she ; no one knew better how to act the great lady. Her wit had a style of its own—it was at once refined, bantering, eloquent, and audacious in the choice of words. She had taste. She gave her patronage to Lulli and encouraged Racine and Quinault."

She was the queen of another great fête which Louis gave in 1668, and which is said to have cost him a hundred thousand livres. It took place just after the Peace of Aix-la-Chapelle had given the French King a supreme position in Europe, and its principal feature was the production in a specially erected theatre of Molière's *Georges Dandin*. At supper La Vallière sat at the King's table with Mme. de Sévigné and the daughter to whom she addressed her famous letters. At a table near by sat de Montespan, and with her a severe-looking woman of determined aspect, dressed plainly but " like a woman who spends her life among persons of quality," certainly disapproving of the sumptuous extravagance, although she may not have shown her disapproval. She was Mme. Scarron, widow of a scabrous poet, governess of the children de Montespan had borne the King, and one day to be Mme. de Maintenon, and his morganatic wife.

La Vallière spent her last night at Versailles in March 1674. Deserted by the King, she had turned to God for comfort, and, guided by the great Bossuet, she had at last found peace. He said of her : " The mark of God's favour is the strength and humility that accompany all her thoughts. He speaks and she obeys." She paid all the visits of ceremony demanded by etiquette, making as it were a public confession of her sin. " Since my sins are known to all," she said, " it is necessary that the repentance should also be known." The King was indifferent, but his kindly Queen was gentle and compassionate, ready with assurance of forgiveness. The sad ceremonies over, La Vallière quietly drove down the long avenue of Versailles into Paris, past the Tuileries and Notre-Dame, to the Faubourg St. Jacques : " Almost opposite the Val-de-Grâce rises a noble gateway framed by two columns. A crowd has gathered, for the news had been spread abroad that on that day the gates would open and then shut on the Duchesse de la Vallière for ever. She had come to the entrance of the Carmel."

Once before she had escaped from Versailles to a convent, to be brought back by the always useful Colbert, but this time she had left Versailles for ever. " When I shall be suffering at the convent," she once said at Versailles, " I shall only have to remember what they made me suffer here, and all pains will seem light to me."

She died after twenty-six years of the most rigorously ascetic life, subjecting herself to the severest disciplines, ruining her health by lengthy fasts, eager to pay the full penalty for her wrongdoing. On the morning of her death she was found by the nuns lying in a dead faint, numbed with cold, at the threshold of the sanctuary, and when she was taken to the infirmary to die a few hours later, her emaciated body lay between sheets for the first time since she passed the convent gate.

The flaunting de Montespan was to stay nearly another ten years at Versailles, but not as the supreme sultana. The Grand Trianon was bought for her, and the King was the slave of her caprices, but, after a time, they began to weary him. Bossuet having persuaded the King to permit Louise de la Vallière to take refuge in the convent for which she had yearned so long, set himself to urge the dismissal of de Montespan and the ending of a public scandal. In 1675, indeed, she left Versailles, but only for a little while, coming back to receive from the King as compensation for her temporary disgrace, a dress of " gold on gold, and gold embroidered on that, and above that again a gold-in-relief figure with gold mixed with a certain gold which makes the most divine material that ever was imagined." De Montespan fell because she nagged. She was foolish enough to be rude in public. Moreover, again there were rumours of dealings with sorcerers, of black masses and those consultations with alchemists in the search for the philosopher's stone to which Molière refers in his *L'Amant magnifique*. The stories were probably vastly exaggerated, if not entirely

THE CHATEAU, VERSAILLES

untrue, but the King was now a man of forty, always jealous for his dignity, which, be it added, few kings more consistently maintained, and he had always a genuine regard for religion. The domination of de Montespan came to an end in 1679 with the short love affair with Mdlle. de Fontanges who, to quote a contemporary, was "as fair as an angel, as stupid as an owl." But this episode lasted for something less than a year.

Already the King was coming more and more under the influence of the widow Scarron ; already de Montespan had grown afraid of "those quiet black eyes." The gradual capture of Versailles by a woman with no mean ambition and whose genuine piety, despite Saint-Simon's sneers, is now generally recognised, is one of the most amazing incidents in royal history. In 1675 the governess of the King's illegitimate children became Mme. de Maintenon, mistress of a wide domain, and possessor of a considerable income. "Mme. de Maintenant," the courtiers called her, setting their sails to the wind. The King was growing serious, and weary of the brilliant "flies" —the word is Mme. de Sévigné's—about his Court. At Easter, before the King made his Communion, he listened patiently to a sermon from a Jesuit who boldly urged him to repent and set his people a good example. "What a charm might it not work on certain disheartened sinners who have fallen back into despair if they could say to themselves : 'Behold this man whom we have seen in the same debauchery as our own, behold him now converted and submitting himself to God.'"

But the complete conversion was not yet, and de Maintenon herself planned to leave Versailles and to live at Maintenon the quiet life of a lady bountiful, spending her time in the service of the poor. But she stayed on through the Fontanges episode, and then, with one mistress dead, and her predecessor permanently out of favour, her undisputed hour came at last. She held an amazing position—nominally lady-in-waiting to the Duchesse de Richelieu, actually the confidante of the King as well as the friend of the Queen, "the machine that drives the whole thing." Her influence was so thoroughly understood by Pope Innocent XII. that he sent her a letter written with his own hand, with the relics of a holy martyr. And her influence was for good. "Never," said the Queen, "has the King been so affectionate to me as since he has listened to her."

In 1683 the Queen died, and very shortly afterwards, though exactly when and where no one knows, the King and de Maintenon were secretly married. The new position was accepted by de Maintenon with a characteristic quiet composure. Perhaps she might have prevented the revocation of the Edict of Nantes, and it cannot be forgotten that she was born a Huguenot. But heresy and revolution were convertible terms in seventeenth-century France, and heresy to de Maintenon was fatal to order. Her solicitude for the King was at times tiresome, but never really resented. Her great work was the foundation of the school for girls at St. Cyr, near the palace. Here is her own account of a day in her life at Versailles :

"They begin to come into my room at about half-past seven. First of all it is Monsieur Maréchal (the King's first surgeon). He is hardly gone out of the room when Monsieur Fagon comes in ; he is followed by Monsieur Bloin, or some other person sent to inquire how I am. Sometimes I have extremely urgent letters which I am obliged, by sheer necessity, to put aside. Then come the more important people : one day it will be Monsieur Chamillard, another it will be the Archbishop ; to-day, some general just departing to the armies, to-morrow some audience I am obliged to give, and that has been specially asked for, with this peculiarity, that these are almost always persons whom I cannot put off seeing, for of course it must be done in the case, for instance, of officers just going away, and so with others. . . .

"Once the King comes, they have to go. The King stays with me till he goes to Mass. I do not know if you have remarked that in the midst of all this I am not yet dressed. If I were, I should not have had time to say my prayers. So I am still in my nightcap. All this time my room is like a church with people passing through it like a procession ; everybody comes through, and there is a perpetual coming and going.

"When the King has heard Mass, he comes back to my room ; afterwards the Duchesse de Bourgogne comes with a number of ladies and they remain while I dine. It would seem as if that time, at all events, might be spent for myself; but you will soon see what really happens. I am anxious to know whether the Duchesse de Bourgogne is doing anything unsuitable, whether she is treating her husband properly; I try to make her say a word to this lady, to see whether she is behaving with kindness to that other. I have to talk to all the company and contrive to bring them all together. If anybody commits an indiscretion, I feel it. I am embarrassed by the manner in which people take up what is said; in short, I am in a state of mental disturbance than which nothing can be worse.

" I am hemmed in so closely by a circle of ladies that I cannot ask for anything to drink. Sometimes I turn round and say, looking at them, ' You do me great honour, yet I really should like to have a serving man.' When I say that, every one of the ladies wants to wait on me, and hurries to fetch me whatever I may want, which involves me in another sort of discomfort and inconvenience.

" At last they go away to dinner—for I dine at noon with Madame d'Heudicourt and Madame de Dangeau, who are not in good health. So I am left alone with them, at last; everybody departs. If ever there was a time during which I might amuse myself for a moment, it would be now, either by talking or playing a game of backgammon. But Monseigneur generally chooses just at that time to come and see me, one day because he is not going to his dinner, and another because he has dined early before he goes out hunting. So after all the others, he arrives; he is the most difficult man in the whole world to entertain, yet entertain him I must, for I am in my own house. If it were to happen in another person's house I should only have to sit myself down on a chair and say nothing at all, if I chose; the ladies with me can do that if they please, but I, who am in my own room, must make myself agreeable, I must find something to say; that is not particularly delightful. After that we leave the table.

" The King and all the Princesses and the Royal Family come into my room, and bring the most tremendous heat with them. We talk, and the King stays about half an hour; then he goes away, but nobody goes except him; all the rest of them are still there, and as the King is no longer present they all draw closer to me. They gather all round me, and there I have to stay, and listen to the jests of Madame la Maréchale de C——, to one person's joke, to another's story; none of these good ladies have anything to do, their complexions are quite fresh and they have idled their whole morning away. But in my case things are very different, for I have other things to do beside making conversation, and very often my heart is heavy over some trouble, some bad news—the attack that was to be made on Verrue, some little time ago for instance; all that is on my mind; I keep thinking there may be a thousand persons perishing, at that very moment, and others in suffering as well. . . .

"To come to the end of my day. When they have stayed some time longer, each person retires to his or her own apartment, and then do you know what happens? One of these ladies is sure to stay behind because she wants to speak to me in private. She takes me by the hand and leads me into my little room, frequently only to tell me a number of unpleasant and very tiresome things. One has had a disagreement with her husband, another wants the King to do something for her, and I have to listen to it all, and the lady who has no love for me does not allow that to restrain her more than any other. I look on myself as an instrument that God uses for the good of others. Ah! How happy a thing it is to leave it all to Him, to give oneself up to Him, to live on from day to day, doing all the good one can!

"When the King comes in from hunting he returns to me again; the door is shut and nobody else comes in. Then I am alone with him. I have to endure his sorrows with him, if he has any, his depressions, his nerves; sometimes he has a fit of crying that he cannot control, sometimes he is not well. He has no conversation. Often some Minister will bring him bad news; the King will sit down to business. If he wishes me to make a third in this council, he calls me; if I am not wanted I withdraw to a little distance, and at that moment I often say my afternoon prayers. I pray for about half an hour. Though the King may wish me to hear what is said, I cannot do anything at all. I learn sometimes, in this way, that things are not going well; some courier may come in with bad news. All that weighs on my heart and prevents me from sleeping at night.

"While the King is transacting business, I sup. But I am not able to do it in comfort oftener than once in two months. I know the King is all alone, or that he was depressed when I left him; or else, when Monsieur Chamillard has nearly finished, the King will send to beg I will make haste. Another time he will want to show me something, so that I am always in a hurry, and then I can only think of one thing—to eat quickly. I have my fruit brought up with my meat, so that I may make more haste. I leave Madame d'Heudicourt and Madame de Dangeau at table, because they cannot do as I do, and sometimes it makes me ill myself.

"After all that, it has grown late, as you will imagine. I have been up since six o'clock in the morning, I have not been able to breathe freely the whole day long, I have fits of weariness and yawning, and, above all, I begin to feel the effects of age; I end by being so tired that the King will sometimes notice it and say, 'You are very weary, are you not? You ought to go to bed!' So I go to bed, my women come to undress me, but I feel the King wants to speak to me, that he is waiting for them to go, or else some one of his Ministers is there, and he is afraid he might hear. That worries him and me too. What am I to do? I hurry till I almost faint away—and you must know that all my life long I have hated to be hurried. At last, there I am in my bed. I dismiss my women; the King comes and sits beside me. Try to think what I feel like there! . . .

"You know my maxim is to keep a curb on oneself and think of others. The great ones of the earth are not generally like that; they never place any restraint on themselves, and it does not even occur to them that others do it on their account; and they are not obliged to them for doing it, because they are so accustomed to seeing everything done to suit them that the fact does not strike them, and is not even noticed by them. It has happened to me, when I have had one of my terrible colds, to be almost strangled by the cough, without being able to give myself any relief. . . .

"The King remains with me till he goes to his supper, and before the King sups, Monseigneur the Dauphin, the

Duc de Bourgogne, and the Duchesse de Bourgogne all come to see me. At ten o'clock, or a quarter after ten, everybody departs; I am alone at last, and I take the relief I need. But often the anxieties and fatigue of the day prevent me from sleeping."

That was life at Versailles! Well might the great lady regret that she was not a nun!

The King was quick to resent any want of respect shown to his wife. A company of Italian comedians invited to Versailles were imprudent enough to act a piece called *The Mock Prude*, in which Madame de Maintenon was held up to ridicule, and they were promptly packed out of the country. Her position was sometimes made difficult by her brother's extravagances and ingratitude, but with common sense and a sense of humour she provided him with a keeper to prevent him from being troublesome. She was the unquestioned mistress of the Court. With Madame, a German princess with a shrewish tongue and an overwhelming sense of her own importance, she had many scenes, but in the end the royal lady was always compelled to apologise and plead for forgiveness.

As the years went on Versailles became a gloomy enough residence. The winter of 1709 was one of unprecedented severity. The rooms at Versailles were cold and draughty; nothing could heat them. The cold indeed was so great that the wine froze in the bottles and bread hardened on the table. The poor were dying of cold and hunger, and deep and bitter were the murmurs against the King. The glory of earlier victories was forgotten when the news came of military reverses, and there was already talk of revolution. Then death came to the royal family, first the King's brother, then his son, and there was the usual talk of poison, and the gloom grew deeper. The *Roi Soleil* had become a silent, gentle old man.

Louis XIV. died at Versailles on September 2, 1715. For days de Maintenon had hardly left his side, indifferent to the whispering of courtiers already hanging on the skirts of the Duc d'Orléans, the coming Regent. The King gave her his rosary. "It is not a relic, it is a keepsake." And in a broken voice he assured her that he was sorry that he had not made her happy, but that he had always loved and esteemed her quality. "What will become of you, Madame,

THE GRAND TRIANON, VERSAILLES

you have nothing," he said. "I am nothing," she replied; "think only of God!" To the little Dauphin, soon to be Louis XV., he said: "My child, you are going to be a great king. Do not imitate me in the taste I have had for making war. Think always of submitting your actions to God." And to the nobles who stood in his room, "I ask your pardon for the bad example I have set you. I am very sorry not to have done all I should have desired to do for you. I ask you to give my grandson the same diligence and the same fidelity as you have bestowed on me."

He commended de Maintenon to the Duc d'Orléans. "You know the esteem and regard in which I have always held her; she has never given me any but good advice, she has been useful to me in all things, but especially as to my salvation." For the last time husband and wife were left alone together and then, quietly and unnoticed, de Maintenon drove away to St. Cyr, where she heard of her husband's death, and Versailles knew her no more. She dismissed her servants, gave away her linen, cut down her expenses, and at once increased her list of pensions. The inflexible woman was now eighty years old. She had longed for peace, but she had lived in the great world, and she soon found life in the convent dull and boring. But she did not waver. At six every morning she was at mass, and her days were spent with the pupils. She died in 1719. Saint-Simon maligned her, Voltaire sneered at her, but she was a very great woman, who played her part in the drama of royalty with single-hearted courage.

One incident only broke the monotony of de Maintenon's life at St. Cyr. In 1717 Peter the Great was staying in France, and the Trianon was given to him for a residence. Peter was a thrifty soul. "The Czar, being at Versailles and Trianon, sent for sixteen musicians, who entertained him for four days, especially in the evening until three or four o'clock in the morning: at the end of which time he sent them back to Paris without having paid them anything." During his stay he visited St. Cyr. De Maintenon says in one of her letters: "The Czar arrived at seven o'clock; he sat down beside my bed and had me asked whether I was ill. I answered that I was. He had me asked the nature of my illness. I replied 'A great age with a weak constitution.' He did not know what to say to me and his interpreter did not seem to hear me." Peter was very anxious to have a good look at the old lady who had played so great a part in the governing of France, and he suddenly gave an order in Russian that the hangings of her bed should be opened. She blushed a little and then gave her little characteristic scornful smile.

The fashions at Versailles were very curious in the reign of Louis XIV. Saint-Simon tells us :

"The hair was drawn over an edifice composed of wire, and adorned with ribbons and all sorts of appendages, the whole being more than two feet high, so that a woman's face seemed to be in the middle of her body : even old ladies wore it just in the same way, only with black gauze instead of ribbons. Directly they moved the whole edifice trembled, and it was extraordinarily inconvenient."

Versailles was abandoned during the Regency, but Louis XV., a mere boy who had just attained his majority and was married to Marie Leczinska, set up his Court there and it became the favourite royal palace until the Revolution. Louis, "The Well-Beloved," far more than Voltaire or the encyclopædists, was the father of the Revolution. An idle autocrat, jealous of his prerogatives, "incapable of thought or feeling," his long reign was one long story of disaster. India was lost, Canada was lost, and the piling up of taxation to meet military expenditure and royal prodigality excited resentment against an absolute rule that had grown incapable, and the anti-royalist sentiment was stimulated by the writings of philosophers.

La Pompadour, of whom I have already written, first appeared at Versailles in 1745 at a masked ball, and she was soon installed there in a small suite of rooms looking out on the northern parterre and consisting of an anteroom, a bedroom, a dining-room and a pantry. Louis was a shameless debauchee, and long before the death of Pompadour he had started the series of notorious incidents in the house known as Parc aux Cerfs in the Rue St. Médéric in the town of Versailles. Here favourite succeeded favourite, all young, all girls of the people, one the daughter of a cobbler, another of a bankrupt grocer, and so on. It was a vulgar, vicious king who followed the great Louis at Versailles. He neglected his wife and household. He snubbed his four unfortunate daughters whom, with exquisite politeness, he nicknamed Sow, Rag, Scrap and Bad Silk. Truth to tell, they could not have been attractive women. Adelaide was passionate and haughty; Victoire was lazy and self-indulgent; Sophie was extraordinarily ugly; the best of them, Louise, escaped to the convent of the Carmelites at St. Denis near the burial-place of the French kings, and there she stayed until she died. She was pious and intelligent, but with all the Bourbon imperiousness. Her last words were: "To Paradise, quick, quick, full speed," as though she were giving orders to her coachman.

Du Barry, the last of the King's mistresses, made her first appearance at Versailles in 1769. She was the daughter of a sempstress, and had been a milliner, and afterwards a gambler's decoy. With du Barry royal harlotry at last became ridiculous. De Montespan was a *grande dame*; La Pompadour was a woman of character; du Barry was just a harlot, and, when she was installed at Versailles, autocracy grew vulgar. She insisted on attending the meetings of the Council and would perch herself on the arm of the royal chair, as Madame Campan tells us, "playing off all sorts of childish monkey tricks calculated to please an old sultan." She insisted on reading confidential State papers, and once in a fit of temper threw a bundle of them on the back of the fire.

It was at the Versailles of du Barry that Marie Antoinette, a girl of fifteen, daughter of the heroic Marie Theresa, arrived in 1770—the palace gloomy, the King a vicious old *roué*, her husband a melancholy *dévot*. The panic on what is now the Place de la Concorde was the first of the many tragic incidents of her married life. At Versailles the girl was lonely and unhappy, though the people were charmed by her beauty and would go out on a Sunday from Paris to Versailles that they might catch sight of her.

Louis XV. died of smallpox in 1774. Du Barry had stolen away from the palace a fortnight before, "unclean yet unmalignant not unpitiable thing," as Carlyle calls her, to finish her life on the guillotine. It was feared that the King's funeral might be made a scene of public rejoicing, so with little or no ceremony his body was hurried away from Versailles to its burying-place at St. Denis.

The Petit Trianon at Versailles is particularly associated

with Marie Antoinette. It was built by Louis XV. during the Pompadour regime and du Barry used it for the supper-parties which half-fed Paris denounced as orgies of dissipation, though they appear to have been comparatively harmless. There was a merry-go-round on the lawn and a model village at the end of the garden, for even the Court had been influenced by Rousseau and suffered from the fashionable yearning to return to nature. It was in the grounds of the Petit Trianon that Marie Antoinette gave a much-discussed fête to her brother, the Emperor Joseph II., who, during his visit to Paris, shocked the Court with very candid criticisms of the government of France. Here, too, Gustave III., King of Sweden, was entertained at vast expense and again to the scandal of poverty-stricken Paris. It was at the Trianon that Marie Antoinette incurred the condemnation of the censorious by acting in Beaumarchais' *The Barber of Seville* and other plays. It was at the Petit Trianon that she first learned of the plot of the diamond necklace, for it was here that Bohmer, the jeweller, came to beg her to pay for the jewel that she had never seen. The whole thing was a clumsy, vulgar plot, but it was one more blow at the prestige of the Crown, and in stimulating the resentment of the people it hastened the Revolution that was to begin four years later. Carlyle has magnificently summarised the unutterable business in a paragraph :

"Red-hatted Cardinal Louis de Rohan ; Sicilian jail-bird Balsamo Cagliostro ; milliner Dame de Lamotte, 'with a face of some piquancy' : the highest Church Dignitaries waltzing, in Walpurgis Dance, with quack-prophets, pickpurses and public women ; a whole Satan's visible world displayed ; working there continually under the daylight visible one ; the smoke of its torment going up forever ! The Throne has been brought into scandalous collision with the Treadmill. Astonished Europe rings with the mystery for nine months ; sees only lie unfold itself from lie ; corruption among the lofty and the low, gulosity, credulity, imbecility, strength nowhere but in the hunger. Weep, fair Queen, thy first tears of unmixed wretchedness ! Thy fair name has been tarnished by foul breath ; irremediably while life lasts. No more shalt thou be loved and pitied by living hearts, till a new generation has been born,

THE PETIT TRIANON, VERSAILLES

and thy own heart lies cold, cured of all its sorrows. The Epigrams henceforth become, not sharp and bitter; but cruel, atrocious, unmentionable. On the 31st of May 1786 a miserable Cardinal Grand-Almoner Rohan, on issuing from his Bastille, is escorted by hurrahing crowds: unloved he, and worthy of no love; but important since the Court and Queen are his enemies."

It was in the Salle des Menus at Versailles on May 5, 1789, that the sittings of the States-General were opened, Marie Antoinette appearing for the last time in her life in her regal robes. The outstanding figure of the assembly was Mirabeau, whom Madame de Staël, the daughter of Necker, then a young girl, noted with approval as he walked proudly in the procession that preceded the meeting. It is said that during this meeting at Versailles Mirabeau offered to barter his revolutionary enthusiasm for a foreign embassy, but the tale is incredible. Among the Deputies, too, was Robespierre, making his first unregarded entry on the public stage, and the Abbé Sieyès, soon to be known to fame as the master-maker of Constitutions, while sitting among the clergy was Talleyrand-Périgord, the Bishop of Autun. Marie Antoinette was pale-faced and her hair was already turning grey. She had forebodings of what was to happen.

On the morning of June 20 the Deputies assembled to find the doors of the Salle closed against them. Leaving the palace they went to the tennis court in the Rue St. François, and there took oath not to break up until the Constitution had been made and accepted.

On October 5 the women of Paris, hungry and angry, led by "brown-locked demoiselle Théroigne," marched from Paris to Versailles. The National Assembly was discussing the order of the day when Mirabeau startled the President with the statement: "*Paris marche sur nous*." Lafayette, always constitutional, would have stopped the march of the women, but the grenadiers of the Guards bluntly declared: "We cannot turn our bayonets against women crying to us for bread." Soon the women, weary and bedraggled, were before the palace, demanding bread and speech with the King. The King saw five of them, talked to them kindly, promised them food. They came out beaming, only to be sent back again to demand the promise in writing. But nothing happened, and hungry and weary, and ever growing angrier, they broke into the meeting of the Assembly with the demand, " *Du pain et pas tant de longs discours*."

Night fell. The King and Queen were fearful and half inclined to follow the prudent royal princes already in exile. Outside the palace still stood the crowd of damp misery, until at last the Assembly decreed that bread should be sold at eight sous the half-quartern, and butchers' meat at six sous the pound. Then some of the women began to drift back to Paris. But not all.

At midnight Lafayette arrived. The Court crowded round him, eager for his advice, the Queen alone showing courage and calmness. Everything seemed quiet, and Lafayette went to the Hôtel de Noailles near the palace. At half-past four the mob, however, attacked the palace, apparently intending to assassinate the Queen, and lest worse might befall, the King pledged his word to move the Court from Versailles to Paris.

The royal family started at one o'clock the next day, never to return, surrounded by a crowd of shrieking revolutionists who carried the heads of two murdered soldiers at the top of poles. It was six in the evening when they arrived at the Hôtel de Ville, the King assuring the Mayor that he always came with pleasure and confidence among his good people of the city of Paris. And from the Hôtel de Ville they went on to the Tuileries.

Versailles had been the scene in which the drama of France had been set for a hundred years, but after the sad procession of King and Queen with their howling escort had passed out of sight, Versailles remained just a park and a *musée* almost for another hundred years.

On October 5, 1870, the King of Prussia with Moltke, Bismarck and his staff arrived at Versailles. Sedan had been won, the Second Empire had come to an end, and the siege of Paris had begun. The King took up his residence at the Préfecture, not at the château, and his staff were quartered in various houses, eating at the famous Hôtel des Reservoirs. For a while there was some hesitation as to whether Paris should be bombarded or not, and Bismarck was furious with the suggestion that he opposed the bombardment because of the works of art in the city. Such weakness was not for the man of iron. "I think nothing in Paris would give me a transient desire to spare it if I considered the bombardment right from a political and military point of view." On January 18, 1871, in the Galerie des Glaces in the Palace of Versailles the Hohenzollern German Empire was proclaimed, the old Kaiser Wilhelm standing surrounded by his victorious Marshals and the other German sovereigns while the trombones sounded and "Now thank we all our God" was lustily sung. Five weeks later, on February 26, the treaty that gave Germany Alsace and Lorraine and a war indemnity of five milliards of francs was signed in Versailles in a room in the house where Bismarck was living, by five German plenipotentiaries and by Thiers, the little spare man of shrewd common sense, and Jules Favre, the rather shaggy demagogue, who five months before had uttered the famous declaration, "*Pas un pouce de notre territoire, pas une pierre de nos forteresses.*" That was the day of humiliation.

Again the scene is Versailles. Again the Galerie des Glaces where the Hohenzollern Empire had begun. On a brilliantly hot Saturday in June 1919, on a raised dais surrounded by a crowd of eager onlookers, the representatives of the Allied Powers and of Germany signed the second Treaty of Versailles which the Government of the German Republic had been compelled to accept. The representatives first of the Great Powers and then of all the little Powers, including Liberia, solemnly signed their names—a long and dreary business—and then the two Germans, Herr Müller, thin and long, looking rather like a village schoolmaster, and Herr Bell, short and stout and prosperous, both strained-looking and weary, signed away all that Bismarck had won. Afterwards I watched from the windows of the Salle the acclaiming crowds wildly cheering Clemenceau and Wilson and Lloyd George, while Herr Müller and Herr Bell slipped quietly and sadly into their car and drove away.

That was the day of triumph—and men are already asking if the triumph was worth while.

Printed in Great Britain by R. & R. Clark, Limited, *Edinburgh.*